HOMETOWN TALES
HIGHLANDS AND HEBRIDES

Dear Veronique,

Here's my memoir piece about home and how it travels (islands too...)

-All best,

HOMETOWN TALES is a series of books pairing exciting new voices with some of the most talented and important authors at work today. Each of the writers has contributed an original tale on the theme of hometown, exploring places and communities in the UK where they have lived or think of as home.

Some of the tales are fiction and some are narrative non-fiction – they are all powerful, fascinating and moving, and aim to celebrate regional diversity and explore the meaning of home.

HOMETOWN TALES
HIGHLANDS
& HEBRIDES

COLIN MACINTYRE
ELLEN MACASKILL

WEIDENFELD & NICOLSON

First published in Great Britain in 2018 by Weidenfeld & Nicolson
an imprint of The Orion Publishing Group Ltd
Carmelite House, 50 Victoria Embankment
London EC4Y 0DZ

An Hachette UK Company

1 3 5 7 9 10 8 6 4 2

ISBN (Hardback) 978 1 4746 0881 7
ISBN (eBook) 978 1 4746 0882 4

Typeset at The Spartan Press Ltd,
Lymington, Hants

Printed and bound in Great Britain by Clays Ltd,
Elcograf, S.p.A

www.orionbooks.co.uk

CONTENTS

The Boy in the Bubble

Colin MacIntyre

COLIN MACINTYRE is an award-winning songwriter, multi-instrumentalist and producer who has released eight albums to date, most notably under the name Mull Historical Society, so far achieving two Top 20 albums and four Top 40 singles. He has been voted Scotland's Top Creative Talent and has toured worldwide, including with The Strokes, Elbow and REM, and has played all the major festivals. He has performed live on BBC Radio 1, Radio 2, 6 Music, Radio 4, *Later with Jools Holland* and *The Jonathan Ross Show*, among many others. His debut novel, *The Letters of Ivor Punch*, won the 2015 EIBF First Book Award, and will soon be adapted for the stage. His first book for children, *The Humdrum Drum*, is out now.

Born into a family of writers and storytellers, Colin grew up on the Isle of Mull in the Hebrides but now lives in London.

For my mum, Wonder Woman

Tobermory High School map, top of town

TOBERMORY HIGH SCHOOL

MUSIC

Pupil's Name Colin MacIntyre.

Class ....1A...............

Summer Term 1984

Practical Music	A	B	C	D	E
Ability to use equipment properly.		✓			
Skill in reading musical notation.			✓		
Overall aptitude.			✓		
Written Work			✓		
Attitude					
To Teacher			✓		
To Work			✓		
To Fellow Pupils			✓		
Behaviour			✓		

COMMENTS: Colin can get good results, but spends too much time showing off to fulfil any potential he may have.

Tobermory High School music report card

MY TWO WORLDS collided on a wet and windy December night in the mid-1980s. The mainland came to the island.

Picture the scene: a man is wading in from a little boat to an island in the Hebrides. It is the middle of winter and pitch-black. He has a suit on, but no tie, and is carrying an object high above his head as though he has just won the men's final at Wimbledon. He is travelling back late after spending the week working in the city, as he does every weekend in a whirlwind: a one-man Hebridean Grand Prix. Having missed the last scheduled Caledonian MacBrayne ferry, his car has been ditched and he has been picked up from the banks of Ardnamurchan by a boat belonging to a clam diver. But the diver's boat can't get any closer to the little jetty on the island. The tides are not behaving. That's what tides do; they

7

either behave or they don't. The man is only lit by the light of the boat. The spotlight makes sideways daggers of the rain, casting a spell over the choppy sea, turning black into white. The man is slowly reaching the shore, his drenched suited legs gradually emerging from the sea like Charlie Chaplin from an encounter with a hosepipe. It is Friday night. He is almost home. He is my father. The clam diver is my uncle Rob. The object held above my father's head is my Christmas present, come early. It is not the All England Club's Gentlemen's Singles Trophy; it is a 1978 USA original Fender Telecaster guitar.

We all know about the day the music died . . . well, this is the night the music *arrived*. To me. To my island. You might think from the way I describe the scene I actually witnessed it. I didn't. I was at home waiting for the prize. I was thirteen, ready to plug in. My world was about to change.

Fifteen years later, my father died suddenly at the age of fifty-four, after jogging around a reservoir north of Glasgow, where he was working as a journalist for the BBC. The shock of his death kick-started my music career proper and inspired my debut album, *Loss*. That was my way of celebrating him, what he had given to me; what he had waded home with that dark, wet night.

I still have that guitar, with its unusual finish of light green and cream. I have never seen another like it. I am looking at it now — at the stickers I naively defaced it with in my youth. *SAVEEA*, one says. It was a popular word among my close-knit group of teenage friends. Nothing was ever severe in our world; it was always *saveea*.

The guitar has travelled around the world with me; it has stood on festival stages and in TV and radio studios, been played on eight albums and counting. But I have always looked at it as having come from the sea. Every time I plug it in, I expect to be thirteen. I expect an electric shock. And in a way that is what it gave me when it arrived in 1984 and continues to give me now. It has journeyed with me to the mainland from where it came, as I became an islander among mainlanders, a musician, and then a writer too.

It is never far from me, just as the Isle of Mull is never far from me. I am always an islander, even in London, where I have settled with my wife and two girls. I am constantly surprised that the Thames is not the sea; that the voice over the speaker on the tube is a driver from Transport for London and not the familiar tones of the CalMac ferry announcer; that the Piccadilly line stops are interspersed with warnings to 'MIND THE GAP' and not the availability of trinkets in the ferry shop. And all this then replayed in Gaelic. That's what I hear.

I am a native of Mull, a *Muilleach*, which means I was born there, on the island that sits in the Atlantic as part of the Scottish Hebrides. I was born into a big family of writers and storytellers, a bank manager, musicians and plumbers. And Mull is where (some might guess, although it is never mentioned) my debut novel, *The Letters of Ivor Punch*, is rooted.

Mull has inspired my music too. I have netted four Top 40 singles and two Top 20 albums, mostly under the moniker of 'Mull Historical Society'. It might not have happened without that guitar. And I'm not sure it would have happened had I not stolen the identity of the *real* Mull Historical Society from a poster advertising their AGM in the window of the Aros Hall on Tobermory Main Street. That was in the year 2000. Relations between both bodies have been good over the years, but the original MHS have since added an archaeological arm to their organisation to make a distinction from me: they are the 'Mull Historical & Archaeological Society'. There is a little plotline in my novel that makes out I myself am now considering changing my name to the 'Mull Historical & Archaeological Society' too ... But that story is told in other pages.

These pages contain snapshots of some of the people and events that have shaped my words and music, and moulded who I am. My story is about coming from an island, about how music travels in your head from island to mainland; it is about belonging, but, at the same time, having to leave. It is about how an island – its sounds and melodies, its myths and folklore, the stories passed down from generation to generation – travels with you. The stories that continue to mean something. That we can't let go. I feel the need to offer them to others, whether that be on the stage or the page. I've always felt I do this because I need to get closer to something. Now I realise that something is home. But what is *home*? And how does it travel? And what does it really mean to belong, to *plug in*?

AS SPECIAL AS it was, the 1978 Fender wasn't my first guitar. I need to go back further for that – to when I was six years old. The guitar was a small red acoustic and cost me five pounds. Well, it cost my grandfather, Angus Macintyre, five pounds.*

My grandfather was there when I was born – not, as most of the children on Mull are, in the hospital closest to us in Oban, which is the mainland ferry port, but at 'The Home' in the village of Salen, which was the closest thing we had to a medical centre on

---

*I should note at this point that my grandfather's surname is spelled with the little 'i': Macintyre. That is my rightful surname. The lineage dates back to the eighteenth-century Argyllshire warrior poet Duncan Ban Macintyre no less. But I have confused the ranks. I am the big 'I' because I liked the look of it in Primary 7. Two hundred and fifty years of clan warfare and proud progress wiped out in a singular act of what can only be called capitals envy.

the island. While my mother was doing all of the hard work, my grandfather was pointing his new cine camera dangerously close to the whole affair. In the 1970s, films had been made on Mull starring Anthony Hopkins, Donald Sutherland and Robert Wagner, but my grandfather certainly fell into the amateur category, with most of his films starring Trudy, a cross between a Cairn and a Yorkshire terrier, who was small enough to fit in his suit pocket.

The money for the guitar could have been considered my first overdraft, because my grandfather, a polymath who seemed to have all the school history books confined within his head, was the island's bank manager – and resident poet. (Thirty years after his death he is still known as the 'Bard of Mull'.) The Clydesdale Bank was 'Angus's bank'. Even now some on the island believe the recession wouldn't have hit Mull had my grandfather still been behind the desk, with Trudy in his pocket.

I wasn't daft to go to him first. I remember telling him about the guitar and him smiling down at me with laughter in his watery eyes as he handed me the money. I had quite recently been headbutted and rolled by a fierce ram called McTavish at the Lochbuie Estate on the south of the island, where my father was doing some work with the building firm he had at the time. The ram and I rolled for several rotations and it was my grandfather – suited, his glasses falling from his head – who pulled the beast off me by its tusks. My own National Health glasses were already being worn by McTavish for all I knew. So I might still have been milking the effects of this bout; five pounds seemed fair enough for my troubles. But looking at the note, I couldn't understand how this small piece of blue crinkled paper could transform into a guitar.

The walk to purchase the guitar was my first solo voyage. I walked the note from the bank to my mother's hairdressing shop further along Tobermory seafront, 'Elizabeth's Hair Salon'. From there I headed back alongside the coloured houses: past the Aros Hall, Margaret's sweetie shop and the Treasure Shop run by Daisy Craig, past the yellowest of yellow buildings, the Mishnish Hotel (the local fisherman's hangout), and then up the beginnings of the light-house path. There was a cannon up ahead. We were told that in 1588 it had sunk *The Florencia*, a Spanish galleon that still sat on the seabed of Tobermory Bay. Consequently, we all believed we had Spanish blood in us. My grandfather had written a poem about the treasure. But I hadn't seen any of its gold in the sea or in Daisy Craig's.

Before I got to the cannon I turned off the path and began climbing the steps to the Western Isles Hotel, as my mother had directed. Built in 1882, it is an elegant gothic gift from the Victorians that sits above Tobermory harbour like a castle fit for Walt Disney. Below me, but only visible from the sea, was our own version of the famous 'H O L L Y W O O D' sign: the words 'GOD IS LOVE' painted onto the black cliff face in large letters of white paint. But given my Sunday School career had already come and gone in all of just one week's attendance, my only aim that day was to keep my glasses on my nose and reach the top of the steps, where the owner of the hotel, whose son I was going to buy the guitar from, had been instructed to phone down to my mother to inform her that my mission had been safely completed. Which in turn would confirm I hadn't spent the five-pound note in Margaret's sweetie shop.

With each large step, I felt as if I was getting closer to another planet. The note weighed so heavily in my pocket, I had to keep making sure it wasn't already a guitar. The entrance of the hotel looked so big and wide, it seemed to me that the wood touched the sky. I made myself dizzy in the revolving door. It was like walking into Mr Benn's fancy dress shop or Superman's phone box. I was becoming somebody else. It was 1977 and the rest of the world – which we called 'The Mainland' – was being seduced by the advent of something called Punk. But I felt less like Johnny Rotten and more like Charlie Bucket taking my Golden Ticket to the gates of Willy Wonka's chocolate factory.

Looking back now, it strikes me as odd that my first guitar, which marked the beginning of my journey into making music, should have been enabled by my Grandfather Macintyre. Because the Macintyres are the writers (the warrior-poets no less) of my family. It is my mother's side, the Kirsops, the island's plumbers since the Victorian era, who are the musicians. And it was they who first lit the fire that led me to become a professional musician – which, I suppose, given where I came from, seemed as likely as Paul McCartney ever becoming a crofter. But then the odds weren't *entirely* stacked against me, as there was, in fact, a certain 'crofter McCartney' residing down the coast on our namesake, the Mull of Kintyre.

It was Christmas Day, the year before I got my first guitar. We were gathered in Failte (*Welcome*), my Granny and Grandpa Kirsop's house on Main Street, bang in the centre of the seafront. It was well named because the door was open to all. We were in the dining room – the good room that was generally only used during the tourist season for serving breakfast to B&B customers. Most of the family were wearing festive hats. My uncles Donald and John, two of my mother's long-haired, bearded brothers, were making alien, jaw-droppingly exciting noises with curious black and white objects. Guitars they were called. I should mention I was watching down on all this, as my uncle Robert was doing his party trick of hoisting me to the ceiling. I was slightly terrified but also enjoying the view. Snow was falling on the seafront outside, not a common occurrence on Mull, and some members of my family had darted out to have a snowball fight. Our family friend, old Bessie MacAllister, was even doing a games' forfeit of running around the town clock in her bare feet. But, placed back on terra firma, I was transfixed by the guitars and the strange coiled wires connecting them to black boxes, from which the sound seemed to be emanating. One was a six-string electric and the other a bass. The boxes were called amplifiers. It was the crisp sound of the future.

It was only later – but long before that Fender Telecaster was waded to the island's shores – that I realised my uncles hadn't actually *written* the tunes they'd played and sung. They belonged to people called The Beatles, The Rolling Stones, The Beach Boys, Neil Young, Bruce Springsteen, Creedence Clearwater Revival, Bachman-Turner Overdrive, Buddy Holly (he even had my glasses) and The Band. That was when the penny finally dropped as to why my uncles were the island's plumbers and not living in a Gothic mansion the size of the Western Isles Hotel in the Hollywood Hills. But to me they were gods. They were connected to something from another world. One even Steven Spielberg hadn't shown us.

And so it was, a year later, that I handed over my grandfather's five-pound note and took hold of the guitar. It was smaller than my uncles' guitars and a different shape. But it was the perfect size for me.

Leaving the hotel, I heard a few unwanted notes as I had an altercation with the revolving door akin to the one I'd had with McTavish the ram, but I managed to navigate my way out with both myself and guitar intact. I walked down the Back Brae this time, which ran behind the bank, rather than the Western Isles steps. I couldn't risk being ambushed by the Spanish Inquisition. It was like carrying a body in my arms.

When I got to Tackle & Books, run then as it is now by the Swinbanks family, I turned right and walked all the way along the seafront towards the clock. I heard everything: the cawing seagulls, the creaking of the ropes holding the fishing boats to our island, and, as I got closer to the old pier, the mysterious hairy fishermen squeaking in oilskins. They walked to the tunes of Runrig and seemed to be joined by one long eyebrow. They had maps of the seas in their heads and were named 'Steptoe', 'Cally', 'Winker' and 'The Gimach' (*Lobster*). Everyone had a nickname; it was our way of keeping the mainland at bay.

My dad's nickname was 'Header' because of his skill with a football. I would have liked a nickname like 'Buddy' or 'Elvis', who had died a few weeks earlier on my mother's birthday. My new guitar was shaped just like his, and that day when I picked it up I was wearing a light blue sweatshirt with a picture of Elvis on the front. I loved to rub my hand on his head; it was so smooth. My classmates did occasionally call me Elvis, but I hadn't figured on the nickname that would stick for me: 'Trudy', the name of my grand-parent's dog.

I looked to the only house that could clearly be seen that wasn't on Mull, but it wasn't on the mainland either. It was on Calve Island, which sits, like a slither of otherness, surrounded by hidden lobster creels in Tobermory Bay. Everyone knew the house belonged to Mrs Cotton, who had white hair and rowed into Tobermory for her shopping like a slowly enlarging cotton bud. The fishermen called it Duty Free.

Not wanting a fanfare or a hero's welcome, I decided to take the guitar around the back of Failte, via a secret passageway at Jackie Johnson's, the butcher's next door. I wanted to be on my own with this new part of me. Now I felt like Elvis. I sat on the steps of my grandfather's plumbing workshop, to an audience of hanging carcasses gently rotating in the window at the back of the butcher's shop, and gradually figured out how to play the thing. I decided the best way was to dampen some strings with the fingers of my left hand, therefore leaving the 'open' strings free to ring out the tune that I made by frantic-ally thrashing my right hand, all without losing my glasses. But over the coming weeks and months I real-ised that I had to actually press down on the strings to make the guitar really come to life. My uncles showed me that. They were in The Kinks and The Byrds and The Monkees too.

You might think with all this guitar talk that I am a guitar aficionado, that I run my hands along guitars the way farmers do their prize-winning cattle. But nothing could be further from the truth. I view the guitar, or any instrument for that matter, like a plumber might view a ballcock: whatever noise or movement I can get out of it that says it is working the way I want it to work is good enough for me. It was back then and it is now.

This mixture of music and words, of banknotes and ballcocks, makes me realise the debt I owe to both sides of my family: one for their words, the other for their music. I was lucky.

I also realise what an influence my grandfathers were: one with his hands stained with coins, the other with Swarfega; one keeping the island afloat, the other stopping it from sinking; one for his words, the other for his lack of them.

Because my Grandpa Kirsop, unlike my Grandpa Macintyre, was a man of few words. I wondered if all the words he chose not to speak were left behind at war. He had lost his mother at the age of eight and then fought during World War II from the age of seventeen, namely in Austria and Italy, having lied about his age in order to qualify for conscription. There was a war story we knew about him having been about to leave a building to combat enemy fire, when another soldier put a firm arm across his chest to stop him and ran out in his place. The man was killed instantly. I remember thinking that must be what war could do to you: make you say less. A few drams could occasionally tease the words out of him, but even then not much.

I was finding words, and music, were starting to overrun me. On my new guitar I taught myself to play songs like 'Leaving on a Jet Plane' (I was never going to leave) and something weird called 'Ob-La-Di, Ob-La-Da', I started wondering whether I could one day write songs too. And maybe even books like my Grandpa Macintyre. When I say *I hoped*, in reality, as the years and chords and words accumulated, I found I was willing to sweat blood and tears to make it happen. That it did happen is still quite miraculous to me. But how did I travel from musician to musician-author, from islander to apparent mainlander? From the seafront to uptown? From an audience of slowly maturing carcasses to an audience of slowly maturing people? (Sorry.) Why did I go the way of the sea?

BACK THEN, LOOKING out from the island, we called everything that wasn't sea, 'The Mainland'. The Fonz, Reagan's America, *Top of the Pops*, Thatcher's Falklands, Bobby Sands' hunger strike, Evel Knievel, Andy Kaufman's Latka, Grizzly Adams, Maradona's tight shorts, Tucker Jenkins, Olivia Newton-John's tight leathers, the John Peel Show, the Miners' Strike, Frankie Goes to Hollywood, the virgin Madonna, Quincy, John McEnroe's hair, Björn Borg's headbands – all of these were considered part of one thing, one single mass: 'The Mainland'.

We were different. On the island, we didn't really have to go anywhere for our news, for our shared experiences. We had sheep with John McEnroe's hair.

Even Douglas's, the closest record shop to us, situated in Oban, belonged to the mainland. The shop was positioned directly beside the first traffic light

I ever saw, on Oban High Street. (Mull still doesn't have traffic lights, unless you count the four-legged variety.) It was to Douglas's that I ferried over to buy my first ever record in 1982: Toni Basil's 'Mickey'. She and her cheerleader's pom-poms were from the mainland too, in a place called America. I remember the shop still had newspaper cuttings of Sid Vicious wallpapered across the ceiling. Punk, like everything else, took its time to arrive in these parts. My uncle, Lorn Macintyre, a published author of novels, short stories and poetry for fifty years, used to even call me and my older brother 'Sid Vicious'. Sid was *saveea* too.

I currently live on that entity, on the land of Sid – the mainland. But the storytellers around me growing up, the music of their voices, just like the fury and the possibilities of the Atlantic Ocean, never leave me.

My songwriting developed through my teenage years, when I started recording what would become hundreds of songs on my four-track. And then in my twenties, when my music started to take flight, I found myself supporting The Strokes, Elbow, REM, and others, on tour, as I acquired my musical stripes (or, er, Stipes). With time on my hands on the road, I began to jot down some of the tales I remembered from my youth, making up more along the way. The feeling I had when I wrote came from the same 'place' within me as my music. It made me realise how much my creativity over the years has been influenced by home.

My debut MHS single, 'Barcode Bypass', is about a small-town shopkeeper trying to tell his wife that the new twenty-four-hour supermarket is putting them under. His heart is failing as a result. A small tale that paints a bigger picture. I wrote it in a kitchen in Maryhill, in Glasgow, at the end of 1999, the year my father passed away. It was the eve of a new millennium; I had left university and was working at BT's Directory Enquiries, in a call centre that evoked the setting of Orwell's *1984*. That song changed my life. On its release in 2000 it was named *NME*'s 'Debut Single of the Year' and all seven-and-a-half minutes of it were played by Jo Whiley on BBC Radio 1. Everything started happening for me very quickly after that. I even met an American girl, Pam, a light, who would become my future wife, on the day of its release. It was love at first sight for us both.

London's *Time Out* took me home to Mull and noticed how the 'big' Co-op was quite close to the corner shop on Tobermory seafront, and assumed this location was the spark of the tale. I probably went along with it. I would like to think the song's theme was inspired by being an islander in the city – a small-towner thrust into a world of commercialism and bigness; of people in call centres clocking in and out as though rotating on over-sized mouse wheels – but in reality it might have had just as much to do with the demise of Alf Roberts and his corner shop in *Coronation Street*. Mostly, though, I reckon it was because I sang it in the first person. I *became* the character in the song.

By my late twenties, I had created many more characters in song and I wanted to do the same in a novel, but I knew I needed an authentic voice, which, hopefully, I had discovered within my songwriting by then. I knew I needed to tap further into it, that 'place', which was to go the way of the sea, the island, and my family. My Grandpa Macintyre, the giver of overdrafts, provided the literary spark for me. It was no wonder his family nickname was 'Santa'.

He lived with my grandmother, Betty, above his self-titled bank on Tobermory Main Street, and so the lines between banker and poet were not clearly drawn. He wrote serious, melancholic, often comic, verses about all sorts. Possibly his most often-recited poem is 'Islay Cheese', which was inspired by a story in the

Oban Times. Our bible. It was reported that Islay's cheese was having aphrodisiac powers in Italy – even with the nuns, and in the Vatican too. Everyone was at it! At least that was how my grandfather had it. He also wrote a very funny poem about the *SS Politician*, which sank off the Outer Hebrides in 1941, together with its precious cargo of whisky, inspiring the film *Whisky Galore*. Such cargo did not go unnoticed in those dry times of war: who is to say it was not the deliberate workings of the Atlantic?

His books were on the shelves in the bank flat, but also on the counter in Margaret's and in Tackle & Books, as were cassettes of him reciting his verse. His book, *The Ceilidh Collection*, was yellow and I wanted to make one just like it. He used poetic language even when discussing accounts with his customers, and it seemed to me his voice couldn't get enough of words. My 'homework' was often to hear him recite his poetry, including his 'Ode to Jocky Wilson', which was his tribute to our fellow Scot, the rotund, toothless World Darts Champion. He wrote the poem 'An Invitation to Mark Thatcher', which was his offering to the Prime Minister's hapless son, for him to come and try his luck at the annual Mull car rally, following the news he'd got lost for six days in the Sahara

Desert during the Dakar Rally. My grandfather also performed his poems, such as the serious, beautifully melancholic, 'Memories of Mull', in the Aros Hall, and was appreciated in many other venues up and down Scotland. He might have been the only bank manager who went on 'speaking' tours. After his death at the age of seventy-five, his anthology, *The Compleat Angus*, was published with a foreword written by Iain Crichton Smith.

My own ambition of getting my words published drew closer about five years ago. I heard a voice in my head while sitting on a flight. I wrote down what I was hearing: '*Dear Mr Obama, There were six eggs in the chicken coop this morning, two more than yesterday and four more than the day before. It's official: you can tell your men the recession is showing signs of recovery.*' And I was off. I had morphed into an old man living on an island, a man called Ivor Punch, who turned out to be the island's retired police sergeant. Really, he was a morphing of many of the old men I knew. He struck a nerve. As did the reason why this self-appointed leader of the island was writing to the leader of the free world, who he considers his equal. A whole cast of characters presented themselves around

Ivor, developing a shared story, a kind of uniformity, despite their differences.

In Ivor's voice, and some of my other characters, I was keen to explore a notion I have, now that I have travelled a tad further than the Western Isles Hotel: that there is a global language. My experience of people – whether in Europe, the Middle East, Africa or North America – is that, despite their different tongues, they often speak the same language. It is a shorthand delivery of speech, a directness that is often found in the aged, and often involves humour, and is particularly prevalent in the one-word character assessments of the Hebrideans (often that is a swear). All our hometown tales are probably not so different, no matter where we grew up. People are people, whether in song or on the page. I realise what I am trying to say in my fiction – and maybe in my music too – is that an island life, an island community, can be a world in itself.

But in my mind, Ivor is not the novel's central character, just as, being an islander, often I do not feel the central character in my own life – the island is. And it is run a close second by the Atlantic Ocean. And so this expanse of water also became a character in my novel, providing a symmetry of sorts as two of the island's sons leave the island – one to London, the other to the east coast of America. Both are destinations that have attracted me.

Why do we leave? Do we go in search of ourselves? I have found that islands travel; that sometimes you have to leave home to know what home is. Who *we* are. And I have. I followed the pulls, the currents, the electric shocks that have catapulted so many others like me to the mainland. But so much of me remains on the island, like the sheep's coat caught on the barbed-wire fence.

I WAS HOME on Mull recently, playing An Tobar (*The Well*), Tobermory's arts and music centre run by Gordon MacIean – a man who I've coined an angel with sideburns. The night after my show I needed to send an email, so I drove over to An Tobar in the pouring rain to try and access their Wi-Fi. The building – which used to be my old primary school – was locked, and as I sat on the bench outside, crouched underneath an umbrella with my laptop, I remembered sitting in the same spot on my first day at school. The performance room is actually my first ever classroom, and several years back I recorded a more unplugged album, *Island*, in that room on those same floorboards as my Primary 1 teacher Mrs McNabb used to walk in her red skirt.

As I waited for the Wi-Fi to find me, I looked down at some teenage boys loping up the steep Post Office

Brae with the rain falling on them, only the blackness of the sea behind them. A couple had guitars without cases strung on their backs. I saw myself and my friends. I wondered which of them would stay and which would leave. Watching them, such a tight little moonlit bunch heading towards the orange street light that has always been at the top, rotating in my mind which would be the group leader and which would fall behind, cast me right back to my schooldays.

I remembered how the older boys would often wait for us at the top of the brae at lunchtime, only to carry us all the way down to the bottom again. If it was icy, it was like scaling Mount Everest and would take for ever. I had claimed my own tree halfway down the brae, called 'The Midgie Tree'. Sometimes the boys would take pity on me and offload me there instead. In reality, I felt privileged to be chosen.

Many dark days and nights were spent with my friends after school, on my tree, or gathered at each other's houses, playing or listening to music. The folklore and mythologies of small places are integral even to the young, and we'd often try to spook the other out by telling tales. Frequently there were power cuts and those stories were our only entertainment, often told by candlelight. Back then Wi-Fi wouldn't even have been something *Back to the Future*'s Marty McFly could have foreseen.

The handing-down of stories is of particular importance on an island, where everything and everyone floats. It must be the threat of the surrounding sea that keeps the tales with us, that keeps them alive, bound up in the people and the half-light of teenage evenings.

I recall one such evening very clearly. My cousin Paul and I – we were the same age and in the same class at school, and so grew up like brothers – were perched on our new BMX bikes, riding the Galley Goo Road on the outskirts of Tobermory. We saw something unusual and menacing materialise from the darkness up on the hill. We were certain it was the Headless Horseman. The whole town knew about the Headless Horseman (it would go on to roam the pages of *Ivor Punch*), but nobody I knew had ever seen it. My bike had just arrived on my birthday and I was sure the whole town could hear the brakes squeak. The Headless Horseman included. Word of our sighting spread on the teenage grapevine and my cousin and I were treated like celebrities the next day at school, even though, it has to be said, the sighting was completely unverified by anyone else. It could have been a large fence post or a bite in the land, or even a peat-cutter out on a late shift. Whatever it was we saw that night on that hill – real or imaginary – some twenty years later I knew I needed to write about it. Paul and I felt the presence of the Horseman that night. Maybe we had been watching too many Spielberg movies. Close encounters of a headless kind.

In *Ivor Punch* another of the island's sons recalls how one wild and wet evening he and a teenage friend were visited in their car by an odd spirit, a sort of mermaid ghost. I borrowed this tale from a local man who told it to me and my friends during a black night on the moors as we spectated at the annual Mull car rally. We were waiting for Mark Thatcher to arrive from the desert. Huddled together and swigging a few cans of cider we weren't supposed to have, we were captivated to hear how this man had picked up a hitch-hiker one stormy evening on the Glen road. It is a bleak stretch of moorland that cuts across the middle of the island, more lunar than earthly. We were on the road as he told us: *'It was only after I let the hitch-hiker out of the car again, that I knew what was wrong.'* He paused for a swig. *'The bugger was completely bone dry. And it was pishing down the whole night. The seat where he'd been sitting was dry too.'*

It's no wonder I can't leave the mythology of my island behind – because *home* travels in this way, and the supernatural with it.

I suppose my father's weekly travel routine to various BBC studios on the mainland first gave me an insight into what you could do if you left the island. By the late 1970s he was no longer running his building firm, but, in part due to the actions of a bread van (more of which later), he was instead working away Monday to Friday in the role of BBC Scotland's Political & Industrial Correspondent. Missing him dreadfully would give me the feeling a bubble was building around me. And growing up on Mull, I sometimes felt that the island was just too claustrophobic.

Islands are built on a strong sense of community, but it can at times be a bit like living in *The Truman Show*. The same people in the same places every day. And the mainland had brought me my Fender guitar; it was too big a carrot for me to ignore. Some natives, of course, had no choice but to leave, to war, like my Grandpa Kirsop. And we had the silence of the war memorial, situated just above the 'GOD IS LOVE' cliff-facing, to remind us that some of them never came back.

But an island community is also like having a warm arm wrapped around you, and I wouldn't have traded it for the world – or the mainland – when I was a child. You don't lock your car or your house. Children can roam free. It is a comfort to know from whom and where your neighbours derive, and for them to know the same about you. Shared history is a big deal. And it was my grandparents' generation – the old voices around me as a child – that inspired me and gave me that warm feeling.

I was always fascinated by older people, by what they had seen and by what they had touched. My Uncle Eric and Aunt Avril, on a visit back to Mull from their (to a young child at least) exciting lives in Northern England, often pointed out how the old were like living, breathing history. I'm glad they told me that. They have always been very supportive of me. They both worked in education, were great fun and even had me trying to answer questions such as *who came second in the war* . . .

The central character in my forthcoming novel talks about the best kind of education being at the foot of an old tree. Associating an old tree with an old person. I often had that feeling as a child. There was music in the voices of the old around me, and in their hands too. Particularly as some had been on musical journeys around the world I could only dream of. There was the legendary accordionist, Bobby MacLeod, who, despite being in his later years in the 1980s, still owned the Mishnish Hotel, and who I was told had taken his accordion to New York to wow the Americans in the 1950s. New York! All the way from Tobermory pier! Then there was the legend of 'Pibroch', a majestic fiddler who we knew had tragically drowned in the early 1970s behind the shelters opposite the Aros Hall. There were names of local characters like 'The Dean' and 'Ballachan' too, who were long gone but who still lived on the tongues of the old around me.

One such character who was still very much alive in my youth was an old man called Big Al. I remember him as a gentle, jovial big soul, with drooping eyes and looks akin to the chef forever floundering after The Fonz in *Happy Days*. One morning, when I was eight, I was playing my red acoustic guitar on my grandparents' doorstep near the clock on Tobermory Main Street. I wouldn't have called it busking, but I was happy enough to play to people at the front of the house, instead of to the butcher's meat behind. By now I'd been playing for two years; not only had

I realised that I had to press down on the strings, I could even bend them too. Lots of songs and chords were coming out. The guitar even had a hole in it – where there wasn't supposed to be one – from my boot. But that's another story.

My Grandpa Kirsop came out and performed his usual practice of taking off his flat cap and then replacing it with his big plumber's hands, one at the front and one at the rear. In my mind, I pictured it as the Argyll & Sutherland Highlanders hat he wore between 1939 and 1945, but he never talked about that. He stood above me on the top of the three steps, his hair greased back under his cap. (I once mistook his Brylcreem for toothpaste.) He looked like Fred Astaire and was almost as fleet-footed. I thought he might dance off down Main Street, but he didn't – instead, he looked left and right to see what was happening.

Big Al approached. He nodded down to me. 'Well – is this Bob-whatshisname-Dylan we have sitting here before us, John?'

My grandfather smiled. I smiled. But I knew there was only one Bob Dylan. And he played a Fender Telecaster, not a mini-acoustic with two holes in it. I'd never own a Fender Telecaster. There was too much sea between me and a Fender Telecaster, let alone between me and a global legend like Bob Dylan. The idea just seemed too impossible to imagine.

'Aye, keep at it lad,' Big Al said.

As he spoke, a bit of phlegm jumped from his mouth and landed on my lip. I tried not to react and smiled up at him as he spoke a little more to my grandfather. I was frozen to the step. I wanted to spit, but I couldn't with him here. The behaviour of the town's ballcocks (ballcocks, like tides, either behaved or they didn't), the weather, how many yachts were in the bay – it was all discussed as I sat there not knowing whether to swallow or spit. I couldn't bring myself to lick the spittle off my lip. Maybe when the men went away I could produce a little bit of my own spit and use it to dilute or wash away Big Al's spit?

As I listened to Tobermory's news of the day being discussed at a snail's pace, I tried to tell myself that Big Al's spit wasn't so terribly bad. He was a nice, big, smiley man. I pretended to shape some chords, but all I wanted to do was rub the old man away, which I couldn't do with both of them towering over me. Eventually they said their goodbyes and walked off in opposite directions. I spat onto the pavement. I rubbed the back of my hands on my lips. I did all I could to remove the nice big man. I refused to swallow all afternoon. But this was only the beginning of my troubles.

The next day the town was full of only one sad story: Big Al had died in the night. He was now one of those luminary names of the past. I heard all the adults around me discussing how terrible it was. How much he would be missed. 'Only yesterday Colin and myself were talking to him, right enough...' my grandfather said, a dram loosening his tongue. He, who had witnessed men falling in the trenches of Italy and Austria, and who was once again being forced to confront death. I was pleased to be included as a part of their conversation of the day before, as though I was of value, or even a man like them. It was said how Big Al was a fixture of the town and Main Street would never be the same again. But mostly, all I could think was that I was going to die too. I had Al's saliva. Whatever it was that felled Big Al, I had it too. His saliva was *saveea*. I calculated that he must have died between thirteen and, say, eighteen, hours after his phlegm had jumped from his mouth to mine. I flinched as the town clock struck midday. I only had hours left. I had Big Al-itus.

That evening, I went to Taijutsu as usual, in the

dojo downstairs in the Aros Hall – where, a few years later, I would play my first ever kind of battle of the bands with a rival outfit called Warnings Against Folly, who were *way* more political than my band – and I was sure I was on borrowed time. It was a sunny, quiet night, and as I stood at the white railings in my white gi uniform, I looked down at the white seagulls facing the falling sun like barrel-chested emperors on the last of the white sandy beach, and I was sure it was my last night on earth. Or maybe I was already in heaven? Maybe this was now a parallel universe *above* the clouds. I had the seafront and the quiet of the evening to myself. I had the lap of the waves and the hourly chime of the clock for company. It was my favourite time of day at my favourite place to be, all alone. I tried to put Big Al out of my mind.

I heard the familiar creak of a window being lifted. It would likely be St Peter. I was standing below the flat of a great old lady I knew as 'Merrick', who, back in the normal world, was Ballachan's sister and had a one-legged seagull of her own called Pharic that would land on her windowsill. She lived next door to my grandparents. Every Tuesday and Thursday, just before the strike of seven o'clock (that was when Taijutsu started), she would open her window to me.

I looked up and everything was normal. Maybe I was OK? She was leaning onto the sill in just her bra. She reached out and threw me down a Lion Bar, as she did every Tuesday and Thursday. The bar landed on the empty street below her window and didn't fall through the clouds. I was OK! I ran to pick it up. Surely Bruce Lee prepared for his fights with Lion Bars too.

'Did you get it, Colin?' was the familiar soundtrack.

I smiled and nodded up to old Merrick and then ran along the seafront towards the hall, my yellow belt flailing after me. I was trying not to think that I might still have Big Al-itus. That this might be the last time I would hear Merrick's voice, eat her Lion Bars, be flattened to the mat by my good friend Stewart.

I did wake up the next day. And the next day after that. Taijutsu continued. Playing my guitar continued. I was even thinking about making up my own tunes. I was going to be OK. And something was changing; I was becoming a kind of musician. And soon a guitar like Bob Dylan's would arrive onto the island. The times they were a-changin'. I began sketching stage plots. I had even built my very own personalised 'backstage' area – a hut behind 'Glenoe', our new house. I had a rider of Lion Bars. All I needed now was an actual gig. Oh, and a band.

*

My hut was one of the most popular in Tobermory. Possibly because it was hidden in a dip in the field behind my house, which was the last one on the north edge of town. Therefore, my hut was away from prying, or adult, eyes. Huts were also good places for telling tales. I had another hut that I shared with my close friends: Stewart, Paul, Marcus, Alan, Gordy, Norrie and Steven (or 'MacInnes', which for some reason we pronounced 'MacGuinness'). The hut was a secret from the rest of the town. A clandestine affair, which we named the 'Brussel Sprout', because it was carefully camouflaged using branches and mounds of grass on a wild green patch surprisingly near the school. Someone had *The Texas Chainsaw Massacre* on VHS and it was often discussed there in all its gory detail.

Now I was progressing on the guitar I'd play tunes to my friends in the Brussel Sprout and try to imagine locals passing and hearing this noise coming from the grasshoppers. It might have been considered my first Green Room had I known what one was. But the Brussel Sprout didn't last long. Secrets were hard to keep in a primary and secondary school of only

190 pupils combined. So I put most of my creative energies into my own hut.

If you continued northwards from my hut you would reach the north-east coast of Mull and Bloody Bay, where clans had brutally battled in the fifteenth century, in times before even Big Al or Bob Dylan. My hut was carpeted and the roof was an amalgam of corrugated sheets and tarpaulin. It even had a kind of doorbell. My mum said it should have had its own postcode given the amount of traffic traipsing through her ever-maturing garden to it. Mostly it was littered with Lion Bar wrappers and filled with the sexually frustrated talk of me and my friends. If we'd had our way, we would have constructed it outside the girls' toilet in the Aros Hall. And, in fact, the strategic positioning of my hut was the important thing. Because it was one of only two places I could get a BBC Radio 1 signal. And even then the wireless had to have a coat hanger attached to it. I used to look at the coat hanger as a giant arm pulling us fractionally closer to the mainland. I often listened to Tom Ferry or John Peel crackling down the wire from the BBC, competing with a soundtrack of baaing sheep and neighing neighbours. The only other place I could get a good signal was on a particular patch in our front garden, near where Trudy the miniature dog was now buried.

In years to come, my debut album, *Loss*, would have on its cover a photograph of a dog in a wig. I named it 'Trudy'. I even had a fifteen-foot touring version made by my cousin Julie that you could sit inside. A couple once got engaged in it at an MHS gig at Glasgow University. Around that time I even found myself on the other end of the coat hanger, performing an MHS session live on the John Peel Show, and all I could think about were the huts around the world I was beaming into. I was surprised when John's voice crackled in person.

But back in the hut in the 1980s none of this was imaginable. I used to sit and close my eyes to the music, elbowing the coat hanger, trying to entice the mainland closer, but when I opened the flap to the world there was never a line of girls going all the way back to the edge of the town. I really needed that band . . .

FOOTBALL – ALONG WITH music, friends and family – was a constant throughout my upbringing. The football pitch in Tobermory was more appropriately sloped for downhill skiing, but it was the only way we knew how to play football. On summer nights we would play seemingly endless matches, staying out until we were a black sea of silhouettes trying not to bump into each other, each secretly hoping the Headless Horseman wasn't among us.

Occasionally, a visiting British Navy boat would enter Tobermory Bay and the men would come ashore and find their way to the pitch for a match of *Island vs The World*. Some of them might already have visited the Mishnish bar and we'd end up chasing the combined smell of alcohol and aftershave up or down the slope. It was the smell of the mainland.

My dad was a strong and skillful player but thought

nothing of fighting on the field. Many days and nights I would cringe as he lamped another visiting player, naval fleet, or even family member. But nobody seemed to take offence for long. It was just Kenny, or 'Header'. He once even challenged the legendary Olympic shot-putter Geoff Capes at the Tobermory Highland Games, which was timely, as Capes had just been crowned 'Britain's Strongest Man'.

One time, there was a team visiting from Ardnamurchan. They had a giant centre half who looked more like Mad Max than Mad Max. My father picked him to duel with. After a disputed tackle, Dad bounced up and smacked the man across the face like a kitted-out kangaroo. Thankfully, the final whistle blew and they were separated. Dad walked towards us frothing at the mouth. I was so relieved all seemed to be over. Later that day, we were flagged down by my dad's friend Hughie who said the guy my dad had hit was in fact a black belt in karate and was in the back room of the Mishnish bar trying to navigate his contact lens under his skin from somewhere near his ankle. He was 'gunning' for my dad to 'stiffen' him. But my dad said the black belt didn't bother him at all as we sped off. And I knew it wouldn't. I only had a yellow belt to offer. And a diet of Lion Bars.

When there were big football matches on, some of the town would line the pitch to watch. The local rivalry was between Tobermory Utd, who wore a red and maroon strip like Sheffield Utd, and Tobermory Athletic, in their classic Argentina blue-and-white vertical stripes. The hair was about the same length too.

But it wasn't just football that took place on that pitch; it was perfectly sloped for all our Eddie Kidd and Evel Knievel-inspired activities. It was a ready-made ramp for BMX jumps (and if the Gulf Stream allowed us an occasional winter snow, then tarpaulin jumps too). The mainland had Evel; we had Eenie. Eenie was a nickname – his real name was Iain, although he was also called *Peem*. Eenie was four years older than me and *saveea* in the best possible sense. We had all watched Evel Knievel jumping red buses on TV at a place in London called Wembley Stadium. That was where the FA Cup happened too. But we jumped *people*. And, one night in Tobermory, Eenie went further than anyone had gone before.

The record was twelve boys. The younger you were, the closer you would be positioned to the relative safety of the little ramp at the beginning of the line. That legendary night all the bodies lain alongside each other on the sun-bleached grass numbered a record of seventeen. I was number three or four. As we lay like sardines, I remember looking up at Eenie flying above me on his BMX in Lee jeans and Bruce Lee T-shirt. No one else apart from maybe Eddie the Eagle would ever have attempted such a jump. No one else could have commanded so many willing participants. Eenie seemed to fly to the end of the line. We all cheered. To be alive. The excitement at being almost maimed made everything present, of the now.

Only the equally hell-raising craze of bogey racing could match the buzz of jumping humans. It seemed Tobermory's entire youth was downhill racing on the town's braes in these home-made wooden carts. The one-upmanship involved in the designs was legendary – there wasn't a baby's pram in town that was safe from having the wheels ripped off it for better use. But you couldn't fly in bogeys like Eenie had on his BMX. Even now I'm still proud to have been included in the line-up. News of the record jump travelled like wildfire around the town that night. For several days, those involved felt an afterglow, like we were flying too. It was like living in your own folklore.

But mainly the pitch was for football. Football was my game. It was while standing at the summit of the pitch with friends that I learned a hairy young Argentinian footballer called Diego Maradona had achieved the then unimaginable world record transfer fee of one million pounds – we were astonished. The world was spinning too fast.

In the summer of 1980, I broke a record of my own and achieved 424 keepie-uppies with the ball. I would later, during my time at university in Glasgow, be invited to train with the Scottish League Two team, Queen's Park, at their home of Scotland's national stadium, Hampden Park. I was skilful enough but didn't have enough nous and only lasted for a pre-season, but I knew football wasn't going to be my future. Music was always burning too brightly in my dreams – and their pitch was too flat in any case.

Next to our pitch was the tennis court. Despite the fact the court was an uneven, potholed tarmac surface with sheep marking the lines – it made Highway 61 seem like the Centre Court at Wimbledon – I was like every other kid in Britain when the Wimbledon fortnight came along. We all caught tennis fever and, depending on what year it was, wanted to be Björn Borg, John McEnroe or Jimmy Connors, Boris Becker, Stefan Edberg or Pat Cash. Playing tennis racket guitars, while wearing Adam Ant nose Tipp-Ex, was the thing to do. But only behind closed doors.

Borg was my first love. One afternoon in 1980 I noticed an older boy passing by on a chopper. 'What's the score?' I shouted. 'Tiebreak,' he replied, loping away. I got home that night, having experienced at least one true bounce and my first proper singles match victory, to discover that Björn had beaten McEnroe in an epic too. I lay in bed listening to the yelps and groans of the livestock outside of my bedroom window competing with the sounds of Simon & Garfunkel – who, along with Lennon and McCartney, unbeknown to me, were teaching my unconscious the craft of songwriting – and I nodded in secret satisfaction at both my own and Björn's successes. Five Wimbledon singles titles in a row, and we had done it together. In the dark of the night, I tried to fashion Björn's thin lips, which appeared to be almost glued together, imagining him swatting away the American wasp on the other side of the net. Inextricably, by the next year, I would change allegiances and jump ship – I would be on the side of the sting, of the foul-mouthed American with the Bob Dylan hair and Coke-bottle shoulders. And I wasn't to know the significance of the words as I listened to Messrs Simon & Garfunkel looking for America . . .

The tune on the ghetto blaster sweeping the pitch and the tennis court the summer of 1985 was 'Road to Nowhere' by Talking Heads. The repetitive snare drum at the start of the song was the most unusual thing I'd ever heard. It was almost like a Scottish dance band playing new wave. And was that an accordion in the mix, or was the wind blowing up from the Mishnish Hotel? That summer, after Wimbledon, life became all about one event though – Live Aid. It made my mind up. I wanted to be on a stage. It was like a fever building inside me. I remember running all the way back home from playing in a junior golf tournament and arriving just in time to catch Status Quo kicking the show off with 'Rockin' All Over the World'. It was the same stadium where Evel had jumped the buses. I sat and watched the whole event in the same chair with only my guitar for company. Mark Knopfler even wore a tennis headband. That's what rock stars did. It was so exciting.

As the '80s progressed, I played a lot of tennis with my friend Mark and a couple of bronzed brothers from Australia who were new to the island but who had familial links to Mull. We christened them 'The Aussies'. Even though one of The Aussies was a year younger than me, The Aussies were men, like Pat Cash; we were boys. In fact you'd think The Aussies were bronze statues if you never saw them move. We distinguished them as Big Aussie and Little Aussie – even though Little Aussie was bigger than most of us. They tried to do professional things with our tennis court, like set the net to the correct height, but even they became discouraged, watching in vain as the limp net sagged in the middle below their golden knees. It was more suited to catching lobsters.

Some summer nights, my dad, my brother Kenny, who is three years older than me, my Uncle Garry – my mother's youngest brother who, being only five years older than me, is more like our older brother – and I would drive down to the tennis court to make a foursome. They were some of the funniest nights of my youth. My dad was a gifted, natural all-round sportsman, but, as I've mentioned – and was in fact documented in the many warm and humbling tributes at the time of his death, in both political and sporting environs – he was ferociously competitive. During those summers of my youth, my dad frequently devised new sets of rules, which he cunningly called 'Local Rules' – a collection of unwritten (mostly made up on the spot) jurisdictions that could be employed chiefly and singularly for the purpose of removing hapless tourists off our court. They were usually enjoying a quiet, romantic game of singles, or even a civilised set of doubles, often in full Wimbledon whites. We loved it. Even before we had parked the car, my father, through his peripheral vision, to the soundtrack of Paul Simon's *Graceland* album on the cassette player, would spot these poor unsuspecting mainlanders with white jumpers tied around their shoulders (an actual criminal offence where I come from). They were quite ignorant of the fact they would soon be turfed off the court as a result of breaching a local rule, which, five minutes previous, didn't even exist.

Years later, the tennis court would undergo a complete transformation, worthy of The Aussie brothers' approval no doubt, and almost worthy of the Rod Laver Arena itself. And, along with the neighbouring and similarly revamped, levelled-off, floodlit all-weather football pitch, it now stands proudly in tribute to my father, with a plaque outside each facility: 'The Kenny Macintyre Sports Park

Memorial Trust'. A local councillor, a force for good called Mary-Jean, made that happen. To the extent she even called Tony Blair from her then post in the corner shop, to inform him of the funding campaign. But still, if visiting, listen out for the voice of Paul Simon ... and be prepared for those local rules ...

To borrow a song title from Mr Simon, I was increasingly feeling like the boy in the bubble around the age of thirteen. In part it was because I had more and more music and words circling inside my head, which weren't really part of the external world. I relied on my friends to break me out of it. There was always a new catchphrase on the pitch or doing the rounds at school. '*How's yer lid?*' was a favourite. It basically translated to De Niro's, 'How you doin'?' Although *lid* referred specifically to your manhood. There were others too: '*I shouldn't think so, Jake.*' To this day I've no idea who Jake was. And, '*Wharra head.*' And almost everyone called everyone else a '*tube*'. But nobody called Big Aussie a tube.

The language and stories that formed the island's folklore were helping me escape my bubble too. One time, my friend Marcus and I were sitting with The Aussies on the black rocks along from the Mishnish end of Tobermory Main Street below the lighthouse path. Above us, just visible as the rock face turned along the coastline, were those letters, 'GOD IS LOVE', which we were told had appeared many years before when a visiting minister's daughter had fallen from the coastal edge a hundred feet above and onto the rocks where we were sitting. Somehow, she had ended up relatively unharmed. And so folklore had it that the minister then commissioned these letters. Nobody knew who did the upkeep of repainting them. Maybe it was God himself with a brush?

I fictionalised the story of these letters in my novel, but I never mentioned The Aussies. I remember that day Marcus and I were sitting listening to the brothers talking about their lives 'down under' before they arrived on Mull. Big Aussie, who was a couple of years older than us, told us he could ejaculate so ferociously that it would hit the ceiling of his bedroom. I had never heard of such a thing. Me and Marcus were enthralled but just stared at the sun glistening on the sea. 'Really?' we asked in unison, not turning our heads (though 'How's yer lid?' would have been more appropriate). Big Aussie nodded. 'Streuth,' he said. 'Up it goes every time, mate. It's like firing paint balls right out of your billabong!' I wondered if it was something to do with them having been upside down on the globe. Was it really possible? Maybe it was. What did I know? In almost the same breath, Big Aussie told me my mum was a bit of all right. I turned as pale as the mainland. I decided I'd need to keep a closer eye on the appointments book in the hair salon.

The only thing I had on my bedroom ceiling was a poster of my favourite sportsman of all time, the snooker player, Alex Hurricane Higgins. But he was holding a very different kind of cue to Big Aussie. I wouldn't have known what the word for it was back then, but Hurricane Higgins was all *charisma*. I only truly appreciated the speedy incline of my father's nascent broadcasting career when he interviewed Higgins. Even though Higgins had nothing to do with my father's brief of Scottish politics or industry. I just loved watching Higgins, whether he was playing or drinking. And he drank a lot. He even headbutted people. Each night in our garage I would pretend to be him in the blue light of our Calor Gas fire. We had no street lights on my road, so the window of my garage was like a rectangle of LED light cut into the black night. Higgins was a rebel and in my own secret way – in my knitted jumper and ironed jeans – I felt like one too. I was crushed whenever the man-machine that was Steve Davis beat him. I even tried out some of my Higgins-inspired lunges in the Tobermory Snooker Club, which was hidden in the lane behind Failte. There, Dodo the painter reigned supreme, his baccy tin shaped in the back pocket of his overalls, his legendary one-liners easily matching Higgins' long potting.

Many years later, when my second MHS single, 'I Tried', came out, it featured a video I had made with my mates Alan and Gordy back home one snowy New Year. The video shows me in a battle with a sheep in a bothy (you'd think I'd have learned my lesson with McTavish already). In fact, that sheep, loaned to us by the Glengorm Estate, would be the star, and the first of its flock to get playlisted on MTV. I wanted a particular photo of Hurricane Higgins for the cover art. The 'Barcode Bypass' cover had featured a photo of the Olympian long-distance runner, Emil Zátopek, and so I was keen to keep the sporting theme going.

Back in my garage as a kid I'd watched Hurricane Higgins win the 1982 World Snooker Championships, against all the odds, in a cloud of cigarette smoke and a gust of vodka and orange. As the crowd roared, he repeatedly beckoned his long-suffering wife and newborn daughter to join him on the stage. The crowd was cheering and he was crying, and anyone who has seen the photo taken at the time will know it was a powerful sporting moment and a very human one. It screamed: *this is my last shot at redemption*. When his wife finally accepts his invitation to join him, the seminal snapshot image looked to me like he was saying, 'I Tried'. And so someone at the record label I was with, Rough Trade Records, managed to get Higgins' number.

It rang and rang and then came an abrupt 'hello' that was unmistakably Higgins. He was perfectly civil, but I could barely hear him. He said, 'Mr MacIntyre, that is a very important photograph . . . Wait, call me back in ten minutes and I'll find a quieter pub.' When I called back, he went on to ask for more money than the entire recording and video had cost us to make. 'Two thousand pounds,' he said. That was four hundred of my little red guitars. We could have bought an entire flock of sheep for that. I explained I was just a big fan. I didn't mention the hours I'd willed him on, willing him to win, willing his marriage to work out, or the posters on my ceiling. But the value of the photo just kept going up the longer we spoke. He died a few years later. But I was always pleased to have Alex Hurricane Higgins' phone number, even if I wasn't able to use the photo. I can't bring myself to delete it even now. And I was also glad I never invited either of The Aussies into my bedroom, or my mum's salon.

I USED TO love standing out the back of my house on a clear night gazing up at the starry sky. Being the last house at the top of the town made me feel even more like I was the last star, the last planet. It was the teenager's ego at work. I could get my brain tangled in knots trying to fathom our place in the universe. Where did I fit? Was it part of the mainland too up there? I started to become confused about the sky at night and how similar it looked to the blackness of the sea around us. I couldn't understand how long space went on for, and it troubled me that I couldn't put a fathomable distance between it and me. It all felt too close and too far away, and I found myself trying to join the stars to make something recognisable. There was a face I could see in a tree at the bottom of my road that troubled me as well.

It was as if there was too much space around me,

as if the bubble I was in was expanding and needed piercing. I was becoming preoccupied with things I couldn't see, filling my head with voices and music. *Melodies* – I would go on to realise they were called. But this confusion of not knowing how long the sky went on for or understanding the sounds in my head was bothering me. I never told anyone about it. But it would get a lot worse before it got any better. I couldn't comprehend the rush of activity or why I couldn't turn it off. I felt like somebody had stuck the coat hanger in me – and it was scary. My family were all around. I couldn't walk in the town without seeing one of them. But I couldn't talk about it. Fortunately, I would soon have the distraction I needed. I would be standing on the town's biggest stage. Plugged in. Getting the sounds in my head out. Taking a giant leap. Like Hurricane Higgins. Showing whoever cared to look and listen what was really shining inside me.

Around this time, and shortly after my Fender guitar arrived, I was lucky to win a significant prize at the local coffee evening. On Wednesday nights in Tobermory most of the town descended on the Aros Hall to eat cakes and play games. I thought of us as The Wednesday People. Stalls were set up all around the hall and the town's doctor, an imposing but trusted

Yorkshireman called Dr Clegg, would reign supreme over the tombola. The Taijutsu dojo downstairs was transformed into a cafe.

One night at the tombola I won an old record player. It was grey and came in a sort of suitcase. It could fold up, like the one Elvis had listened to his first acetate on. And I won three records with it: Queen's *Greatest Hits*, *With The Beatles*, Simon & Garfunkel's *Sound of Silence*, and also a box set of American classics from each year of the 1950s. That night I fell asleep with the needle finding the groove of 'Tell Laura I Love Her'. Now I had tunes spinning in my bedroom as well as in my head. And band discussions were underway. But then I had something bigger to worry about.

Mum was never ill. Some of my school friends would also say she looked like Wonder Woman. But even more than looks, she had the stamina and work ethic of Wonder Woman. A colleague of my father's at the BBC once visited Mull and told us his tale of stepping off the ferry at Craignure looking out for the shy, retiring island woman he imagined must be married to Kenny Macintyre, who my dad had arranged would pick him up, only to be met by this dark-haired beauty revving her fuel-injected red Escort.

Mum had looked after the island's hair since she was sixteen, without a break, even when she got married and had us. And when her husband began working away off the island Monday to Friday, she managed to juggle everything, never missing a day at the coalface or a parent–teacher night.

But one day towards the end of that year of Live Aid she was taken to her bed. It was completely out of character, and went on for weeks. It was decided to move her down to my grandparents' house on Main Street so she could be looked after better. My brother and I moved down with her. My Granny Kirsop was like a second mother to us and so it was a comfort to be there. I was fourteen and beginning to realise what a rock Mum was for us all, for the entire family, given she was the oldest of six. Something clearly wasn't right.

Eventually, on Christmas Eve, it all came to a head. I heard talk of an ambulance to take Mum to the ferry. I walked out of my grandmother's house and along Main Street towards the Lochinvar, a cafe owned by Marcus's family, which stood at the foot of the Post Office Brae. It was a popular hang-out and one drink in particular was legendary: a tall glass of Coke with an ice cream ball dropped in. I had never experienced anything like it – you felt you were diving into a sea of candy. Every part of you tingled when you drank it and your tongue felt like it was the only tongue in the world.

That's where I went the day I knew my mum was so ill she would have to leave the island. I wasn't sure if she was dying. I felt guilty for sneaking off, but I didn't want to be there, to face the fact she was leaving. The next day was Christmas and I didn't want to face that either.

The drink didn't hit me in the usual way, but I took as long as I could to finish it. Eventually, I looked at the clock next to the posters of rams' heads on the wall and figured Mum would have left for the ferry by now.

I left the cafe and walked out onto Main Street. It was a surprisingly sunny but seasonably cold day. The sea was choppy and on the tongues of the last-minute shoppers. As I passed the Co-op, I could see an ambulance positioned on the street outside Failte. I stood opposite the Christmas tree at the town clock and watched a flurry of my family members going in and out of the house. My Granny Kirsop looked as pale as the sky.

I walked a bit further and stopped outside Richard the butcher's. I saw the ambulance men carrying out a bed and on the bed was a body in white sheets. I saw her flash of jet-black hair. It was like watching a film or a mother in somebody else's life being carried just thirty or so yards away from me. I didn't want to walk too quickly or to move at all really, because then what I was watching would be real. If I lingered out of sight for a minute or two longer, I could try to convince myself that Mum wasn't ill or about to leave the island. I walked slowly enough so that by the time I reached Failte the ambulance was already on its way along the seafront. I half expected it to drive straight onto the sea. I stood, not knowing whether to go inside or keep walking after it. The ambulance turned up the Back Brae and disappeared out of sight. The next day, Christmas Day, we learned that mum had pleurisy.

As 1986 progressed, despite treatment, it was clear Mum still wasn't herself, but the year was to be remembered for another reason. One day late in May, we got a call. My brother and I were out in our garage playing snooker. Our garage was a local hub of snooker and darts competitions, with league tables hanging from the back of the door. The call was from Granny Macintyre. My grandfather was in the toilet and not responding. He had had a series of strokes since the early eighties and we feared the worst. We drove down with Mum to Main Street, and Granny's voice said, 'Right . . .', as normal, through the intercom as she buzzed us in. We bounded up the steps to the bank flat. But nothing was as normal.

My brother and I got into the bathroom, lifted my grandfather and carried him through to the bed. He wasn't saying anything or shouting his usual refrain of 'Betttyyy!', or moving at all. Soon Chris Swinbanks, the nurse, arrived and searched for pulses and did further checks. Then she placed a mirror at my grandfather's mouth. She waited several seconds and turned to my grandmother and said, 'I'm so sorry, Betty.' I can still see her empathetic face. She lived only a few doors down. My grandfather – together with all his words, all his words written for my grandmother – was dead. Soon the whole island would know.

In the days that followed, a new poem was discovered. My grandfather had written it the day before he died. It was called 'Taynuilt Safari'. It was a beautiful tribute to the landscape of the village outside

Oban where he was born and raised, and it was also a tribute to my grandmother: *'Of course you'll come with me my Queen, For old men risk a fall . . .'* I decided to put that line into a song of my own, and many years later it inspired me to record a song for my third Mull Historical Society album called 'Tobermory Zoo'. I was proud to have carried him that day.

For a while after his death it felt that all I had of him were photographs: one of him standing next to my stylish grandmother on their wedding day in 1940, and next to it, one of him grinning alongside Robert Wagner. No longer would the bank flat be filled with the cries of 'Betttyyy!' It seemed as though all the history books had gone with him too. But the biggest indication the world had changed was that my father's weekly travel routine was broken. He arrived home to the island that Monday night, having only left for work earlier that morning. He never did that. I felt a huge sense of relief. Later that night there was a Bond film on TV but Dad just stared blankly at it.

I remember the next day my English teacher, Mrs Methven, said in front of the class that I might not be feeling myself and didn't need to complete the reading tasks, and that I should take it slow, and for all the class to appreciate that. She reminded me my grandfather had left his poetry, and that was a comfort.

That night, BBC Radio Scotland broadcasted a recording of my grandfather reading one of his poems, 'Memories of Mull'. The town had lost its bank manager, its bard, 'Santa', and I had lost one of my champions and a head full of the most amazing stories.

When the day came, I found that I couldn't go to his funeral in Oban. Too much of me didn't want to believe he was gone. I remember the whole town seemed to leave (as they would again only thirteen years later for my father's funeral), but on this occasion I wasn't one of them. I regretted that.

I knew I had been lucky to have had precious time with my grandfather in his later years. I would sit with him after school while my grandmother went out to get the shopping. She would always be back 'presently', instead of soon. Somebody had to be with the old man at all times. Or, alternatively, my grandmother would send me out with a brown envelope with her flowing script on the back listing her messages. I never left the bank flat without a pound or two for my troubles. Mostly I would be sent on important missions to Browns' the ironmongers to have her soda water bottles filled by a man called Willy Harley, who also, at some unseen time, had the secret job of winding up Tobermory town clock. Or to Margaret's sweet shop, which Margaret had run for over fifty years and for whom my grandfather did the shop's accounts over discussions in Gaelic.

But now his voice had been taken away. No more would he ask me to put his Josef Locke records on the turntable that was hidden inside a long sideboard in the alcove overlooking Tobermory Main Street. No more would my grandfather accompany Josef Locke in a singing voice that confirmed for me these were the warrior poets in my family and not the musicians.

I remember one of those afternoons with him in particular. He was in the middle of one of his famous World War II soliloquies (when this most jovial, warm and welcoming of men would demonstrate a reason for dismantling the people of every nation on the planet, even the Canadians), and on my way back from the toilet I noticed a little bird was rattling about in the skylight. It had got in through the kitchen window that backed onto the Back Brae. 'What the hell's that?' my grandfather shouted.

This was the moment I knew I had a bird phobia. I turned and ran out of the flat and back down the bank steps, leaving the old man on his own with the bird. I felt so guilty about it – and did for many years after he died. I'd left him in distress and he could have fallen or worse if he had tried to deal with it himself. Luckily, I met my grandmother on the stairs and when she heard my grandfather shouting she bolted inside. Seeing the imposter, she grabbed one of the orange fishing nets on a stick that stood outside her front door all year round, waiting for our younger cousins. I watched as she tried to scoop the bird from the skylight. It was like she was fishing in heaven. She was a blur of red lipstick and she still had her good mac and hat on. My grandfather, by now getting confused – who himself would sometimes practise fly-fishing from his bed – provided the soundtrack of, 'Betttyyy! Betttyyy!'

I can smile now, but at the time I was disturbed. I would go on to write an MHS song entitled, 'Pigeon Fancier (By Correspondence)'. And whenever I perform it I can't help thinking of that afternoon I bailed.

The fallout of my mother's pleurisy, and also the shock and emotional upheaval caused by my grandfather's death, sent my mother's immune system into decline. Now she was frequently bedridden. Wonder Woman wasn't supposed to be laid up in bed. She was fatigued in a way I had never seen before and could barely get out of bed to go to the toilet. And with my father working away all week, I had more household chores to do, including the steady stream of hairdressing towels from Mum's shop. The drying line behind our house was seldom without these blowing rectangles of yellow, blue and orange. Sometimes I would even find clothes pegs in my pocket at school.

As the weeks and months passed, I couldn't avoid what was happening to my mum even if I had wanted to. Eventually, she was diagnosed with ME. Over time, she responded well to homeopathic medication and gradually regained her strength. Thankfully, in the subsequent years, she has not experienced too many relapses and even now, in her late sixties, she runs her own successful country hotel. Linda Carter's cape remains on a loose peg. But I'll never forget that moment when I couldn't face approaching the bed being carried horizontally out of my grandparents' house; when I couldn't bring myself to catch up with the ambulance on Tobermory Main Street.

MY FIRST MEMORY of a disco was in the Aros Hall. I was about six. My dad used to man the door and the most exciting thing was that the back wall of the hall had films of spacemen and planets projected onto it. It was like the sky had slipped. Two-Tone was the soundtrack. The Specials' ska trot was the dance to master. It looked more like a communal wee-wee dance. Much too young, we were. Before then, I had only heard music coming from my brother's or Garry's bedrooms. But Eddie O'Donnell was up on the stage, hidden behind four stacked flashing disco lights, playing the records we were trotting to – and suddenly I felt I was here. Really here! The planetary projections were massive. I didn't know there were other worlds hidden inside the Aros Hall.

Apart from the wall projections, the only real films I had seen by the time I was seven were shown in the cocktail bar in the Mishnish: films like *Watership Down*, starring bunnies, *Firefox*, starring Clint Eastwood, and *Superman*, starring a man with glasses like me. There was one other place to see a film and that was in a man called Pitman's front room in Dervaig, a sleepy village about nine miles from Tobermory on the way to Calgary Beach on the island's western Atlantic coast.* Dervaig is where the McCrone footballing dynasty come from. They once beat Tobermory Primary School 47–3. In the early '80s I saw *Jaws* at Pitman's when the rest of the world was enjoying *Jaws 3*. Now, knowing a tiny bit more about fashion and fads, I realise we were so late on things we were almost early. I couldn't dip my toes in at Calgary for about a year without seeing those giant fangs and hearing that stabbing cello.

At this time, until I was eight, my family lived in a house called Kirk Cottage, which was the closest in the town to the graveyard, my bedroom being the nearest room. I was practically nudging the dead. We spent

---

* The outlook from Calgary is stunning – nothing but sea until North America. I once walked around some old settlements there with the *Guardian* newspaper and the Mull Historical & Archaeological Society. It's also where I got married and remains my favourite place in the world.

many summer days running through the graveyard and I remember one grave for an 'Unknown Sailor' that always had a small basket of plastic flowers by it. The years *1939–1945* were inscribed on the stone with the words 'Known Unto God'. Even though most of my ancestors were buried in this cemetery, I was drawn to this little stone. The grave belonged to a German sailor who had washed up on the island during World War II and was then buried by the locals. I stored the story away and will write about it in my new novel.

While 'Glenoe', our new house, was being built in a field at the top of the town, which would be bigger and have views to the sea (and Mrs Cotton), we decamped to my Gran and Grandpa Kirsop's house on Main Street for a spell. It meant I could finally get my hands on Garry's record collection: ELO, David Bowie, *Saturday Night Fever*, *Grease*. It was like a sonic world opening up. The only downside was that our bedroom was now next to the town clock. Slowly I got used to the twenty-four hourly chimes and the dark mornings climbing *up* the hill to school instead of running down.

One morning, I was woken by my brother and uncle and told that I'd slept in. I just about peeled open my eyelids to see it was dark outside, but then that wasn't unusual in winter. I could hear the fishing boats gently waking up too. 'Is it *morning*?' I croaked. 'Yes,' they said. I got myself dressed and rushed to get my school bag. I did wonder why they stayed in their beds, cosy under the duvets, but B.A. Robertson's 'Bang Bang' was playing – the sound of our mornings – so I didn't suspect anything was amiss. I walked downstairs to get my breakfast and the four hundred hankies my Granny Kirsop would make sure we had before leaving the house every morning. But she wasn't there. Then I heard the clock chime two. I knew it wasn't two in the *afternoon*; unless, that was, Willy Harley was responsible for winding up the sun too. They'd tricked me. I climbed back up the stairs to a welcome committee of laughter. *Bang bang!* I pointed with my fingers.

I didn't know then that I'd write about the clock and how it was commissioned by Isabella Bird, the travel writer and explorer, who had it built in the memory of her younger sister, Henrietta. The one who never went on worldly travels. It was she I became more interested in.

A couple of years after my first disco experience, it was Lynn O'Donnell's birthday party. Lynn was the sister of DJ Eddie. I was eight and she was five years older than me. AND I HAD AN INVITE. Really it was because she was friends with Garry. I had always hung around with the older boys: Garry, Kenny, Roland, Douglas Bowman and others. I wanted to be Dougie. He was cool and his hair did things mine seemed incapable of. But I told myself my invite was on the strength of my vocal cords. Because every school day at lunchtime I would serenade the older girls with a mix of, 'I'm In the Mood for Dancing' by The Nolans, 'Woman' by John Lennon, '9 to 5 (Morning Train)' by Sheena Easton, and 'Psycho Killer' by Talking Heads. The latter obviously must have been reassuring for them to hear from a randy little boy five years their junior. They called me 'Kevin' because I looked like the boy in *The Wonder Years*.

I could also sing TV theme tunes, like those to *Kojak* and *Cagney & Lacey*, and I would practise them first on my great-grandmother 'Tate'. She was the sweetest, kindest lady you could meet, but unfortunately she was unable to walk any more and so she became my audience in her room in the bank flat. She had a history of wearing several hats at once. Born in 1889, she could remember when there were reports of outlaws WANTED in America's Wild West, as well as when Queen Victoria was on the throne. She had been in her early twenties when the *Titanic* went down. Tragically, her boyfriend, and my Granny Betty's father, whom she would never meet, did not return from World War I. Tate's whole adult life had been lived without him. Years later, I attempted to immortalise him and the men who so bravely fell like him, in song, 'Samuel Dempster R.I.P.'. I would do anything to have one more conversation with Tate. She was so happy with my tunes; an ever-willing audience, and every time I stepped into her room I felt nothing but love.

I was looking for an audience too when I arrived at Lynn's party. 'The Tide Is High' by Blondie was booming out of the speakers and I tried to copy the dance everyone was doing, which wasn't Two-Tone any more, but involved flaying your arms in front of you as though you were whipping an imaginary horse. Lynn was with one of her friends, the delicious, deliciously named Donna Hannah. Even Walt Disney hadn't created a Donna Hannah. I pointed out of the window to the seafront and shouted, 'Wow, the tide IS high!' I remember wishing for the words to come back into my mouth, but I was beginning to realise that wasn't possible around the opposite sex, especially while trying to navigate an imaginary horse. I was saved by '(Just Like) Starting Over' and the sound of John Lennon's crisp voice filling up the summer evening.

He would be murdered at the end of that year. I remember watching it on the news; the people gathered in vigil on the New York streets, singing, 'Happy Xmas (War is Over)'. Mum scrunched up newspaper balls into our coal fire as we listened. 'The poor man didn't even get to see Christmas,' she said. He still seemed so present to me. How could he be *here*, but not here? I wondered. Tate died two years later and I had my answer. It was the most silent room I ever walked into.

'MY BABY'S GONE Away'. That was the first song I ever wrote. I was seven years old and wrote it with my cousin Paul. I might have even believed I was 'John'. We sang it into an old cassette recorder on his parents' bedroom floor. I had had the red guitar for a year by then, and Paul was beating on some drums his dad kept in the back of a closet.

Several years passed of my attempted chords and his burgeoning beats and then one day, when we were eleven, Paul got a proper drum kit of his own. Almost instantly, his talent shone. We were halfway to forming our own band. His dad – my Uncle Donald, the first person I ever saw playing a guitar – provided our rehearsal room in the shape of his plumber's garage. Well, it was already a rehearsal room, for his and my Uncle John's group, The Wave Band. It's true we didn't have a record shop, a cinema, or much of a radio signal on the island, but I can look back and appreciate how lucky we were to have this ready-made rehearsal space. All I had to do was run over to my cousin's house, open up the garage door, and an Aladdin's cave of musical instruments lit up before me. Albeit with plumbing pipes acting as tubular bells. I have since been asked my musical influences many times, and I always like mentioning The Wave Band and seeing the confused look that comes over music journalists' faces: *Should I know them?*

Garry was enlisted as our singer and he played guitar too. His impressive vocal pipes were a bonus, and, given he was five years older than us, we figured some of the town's older girls, like his girlfriend Donna Hannah, might come on board with him too. We thought long and hard about the name and decided on TRAX. (Capitals again.) I loved that X. We deliberated over adding 'THE' to the name. Like *The* Beatles, *The* Birds, *The* Human League. But it was decided we would be just TRAX, because it would be bigger on the posters in Browns' the ironmongers, next to 'BED FOR SALE', 'WHIST DRIVE' and 'COFFEE EVENING'.

I was lead guitar. We tried out several bass players. We had our friend Stewart for a day. Neil for a while (who taped the tops of his fingers with black tape like U2's Adam Clayton). We had Mark for a long spell, and then we settled with Gordy, Stewart's brother, who was a year younger than me. We tried out songs by bands my uncles were already playing: The Beach Boys, The Beatles, the Stones, Small Faces, Van Morrison ... and we began adding more tunes of the time, by the likes of David Bowie, Billy Idol, Talking Heads, U2, Dire Straits, The Clash and others. My own songs and singing voice stayed within the confines of my head, behind the safety of my bedroom door, but I knew my hairbrush couldn't be my microphone for ever. I was always obsessed when anything came on the TV about The Beatles. In fact it was Beatlemania I was interested in, almost as much as the music. I liked the way their hair ran forwards and flipped whenever they sang. I liked how girls screamed at them; I couldn't see why this shouldn't happen in the Aros Hall. But it nearly didn't. As our first gig approached, one dark, wet night, after leaving rehearsals I came the closest I ever have to death. Garry and I were involved in a car accident on the Back Brae. The brakes failed and, gathering speed down the steep hill, we lost control and smashed into the corner shop at the bottom. Otherwise we would have ended up in the sea. We were both completely unharmed.

TRAX played their first gig as a support to The Wave Band when I was twelve. I remember being so nervous I even ironed the jumper I was going to wear, as well as the jeans. Billy Idol would have boked. The gig was in the upstairs main room of the Aros Hall, where the discos and coffee evenings were held and where a projected Neil Armstrong had once taken a giant Hebridean step. In the room downstairs, to the power of Lion Bar, every Tuesday and Thursday I was still pretending to be a match for Stewart's Bruce Lee. But this was something different – a million miles from Doc Clegg's tombola.

Saturday night fever: it was past ll p.m., a pure adult zone, the bar was selling alcohol, money was being taken at the door for God's sake. All the town's 'gigs' – for that's what this was – happened late. But as the town clock ticked towards our stage time (did we even have a stage time?), I remember being the only one who was concerned by how empty the hall was. Most of the punters came in from the pubs later. My uncles reassured me 'backstage' that more people would arrive and not to be too upset. All I could think was how much we had practised and it was all for nothing. But I supposed enough of our friends were already in, having been allowed a late pass.

The time came for the PA system to be pressed to 'On'. It was a nervy moment. At the last minute we needed to source a kettle lead for John's legendary 1960s-era bass amp. Fortunately, we managed to borrow one from Iris, an encouraging lady with a red beehive that rose from her head like a flame, who ran the shop downstairs (most of our houses were missing kettle leads).

Due to the hall's pre-war wiring, switching on the PA could fuse the entire island and give you Sid Vicious (or Iris) hair whether you wanted it or not. But all was OK. We plugged in, ready to go. There was a squeak of feedback and a splattering of whoops and applause. We walked to our positions on the stage, like figurines coming alive on my pre-drawn stage plot, and I struck the first bars of 'Sultans of Swing'. It was a feeling unlike any I'd ever had. Not even the world's largest glass of Coke with a dollop of ice cream in the middle could reach the parts being tickled inside me now. I dared not look out to the floor of the hall. The stage was lit by two spotlights, each with blood-red filters, and pretty soon I was regretting the jumper. But I just concentrated on my first solo. And people walked closer.

The hall had filled by the time we reached our last tune. It was an instrumental – 'The Jig' – which had travelled across the sea to us from a band Garry had known in Oban High School, called Freezeframe. Garry played lead and over the next few years it would become our signature tune to end on, after we had segued from Fleetwood Mac's 'The Chain'. People would form circles on the floor to 'The Jig' and gradually spin faster as we played faster. I more than liked how it looked from the stage. I liked being in control up there and seeing the sweat on the punters' brows glistening like Spanish gold.

The gig was over all too soon. My uncles said we had done well. I loved the feeling of applause and also the excitement over the next few days when adults like Pamela Williamson and Dawn Hickford, who used to run our discos, stopped me on Main Street to say how much they'd enjoyed the show. I still felt the glow of the spotlights. I felt like a red Martian – in a good way.

Gigs followed, often in the hall, and sometimes in the school gym. One night, our friend Alan – who would go on to join me touring all over in MHS for the first few years playing bass, and whose dad Jimmy was a good friend of my dad and fellow football player/manager – announced he was our manager. He didn't have a lot of competition, because it wasn't immediately clear how much there was to manage. But a manager was a manager. We even went on 'tour' to play the other villages across the island. All our shows had to have a charity donation and we would post the proceeds and amount raised in Browns' shop window. I wanted to put a sign up for myself: I WANT MORE OF THIS.

The Guitarist magazine became my bible. I would queue up early outside the corner shop waiting for the doors to open, sometimes only to discover that 'the paper boat', which carried the newspapers (most of which seemed to be my father's) and other such precious cargo from the mainland on Sundays, had not sailed into Grass Point due to stormy weather. I wondered if the mainland had finally wised up to the concept of a boat made of headlines.

Despite these hiccups, I was starting to realise I might one day have to leave the island if I really wanted to be a musician. I understood now that some people left to pursue their dreams, like my father, and some stayed. My imagination was taking me elsewhere; I had a thirst for wider horizons. I still had the red glow of the spotlights about me. Was there really Life on Mars?

My uncle, Angus Macintyre, is an inspiration. He is named after my grandfather and is one of the world's foremost mathematicians in his field. He was a fine athlete and is also possessor of the world's firmest handshake and warmest hug. He went from the campus of Oban High School, to Cambridge, Stanford, Yale, Oxford and many other universities as both student and professor. I can barely fathom the CalMac ferry timetable, so I acquired none of his gift. (I recently unearthed my school report card for Physics and in the column marked 'Interest', Mr Brockie, the long-standing teacher, wrote: '*Doubtful*'.) But what I mean to say is that my uncle had to leave to pursue his passion and talent.

I remember the excitement I felt when he and my cousins, Didi, Iona and Duncan, travelled across the Atlantic from their home near the Yale campus in New Haven, Connecticut, to visit us on Mull. I was always drawn to the airline tags on their suitcases. We were the cousins who were always here. We were the cousins without the American accents. Like the

orange fishing nets: we never went anywhere. Yes, it
was an idyllic life, I can see that now, with both sets of
grandparents only a few doors apart on possibly the
most beautiful seafront in Scotland. But despite this, I
sensed there was more out there beyond the sea – and
my family were proof.

I used to trace the map of North America – specifically the northeast part comprising New York,
Long Island, Connecticut – because that was where
my uncle was based. I was obsessed with New York
in particular: Andy Warhol, John Lennon's infamous
Dakota Building, Bob Dylan's arrival there, Christine
Cagney, the films of Martin Scorsese and this venue I
had heard about called CBGB's. America was responsible for much of the music I liked, as well as the ice
cream sodas that were by now making up about fifty
per cent of my body mass. Given I have subsequently
married a New Yorker, maybe it was the future I was
tracing. But the map seemed too big back then; too
big to trace. I got homesick just looking at it.

So I knew that some people left. And some stayed.
But what made you stay? What could make *me* leave?

In my father, I had an example of how to leave without really leaving. Because even when he *was* away, I
could still hear him down the wireless every morning,

lunchtime and evening on the BBC News. The mainland was feeling a lot closer. The signal improving. I even watched David Dimbleby on *Newsnight* one evening introducing a piece from my father about the Miners' Strike. 'Everyone in Scotland knows Kenny,' he said, ad-libbing because of a technical hitch, and it seemed to be true. When Dad died it was documented in obituaries written by BBC colleagues such as Iain MacDonald, and echoed in tributes voiced by leading politicians, that if Scotland was a village, then my dad knew all its inhabitants.

But despite all of this, Dad was mostly interested in reporting the gossip on Tobermory Main Street. And as if his guitar deliveries weren't haphazard enough, his weekly journeys to and from the island were legendary. If he was running late (he was always running late), he would often call CalMac from a phone box to have the last ferry wait for him. That would be unheard of now. One often-recounted story tells of him arriving at Oban ferry terminal to discover the car deck was full. So he ran for the foot-passengers gangplank, his bag over his shoulder, his ure (a large reel-to-reel recorder which he carried in a brown suitcase) under his arm. 'Kenny! Kenny!' he heard as he ran up the steps towards the ferry. He turned to wave and continued up the steps. 'Kenny! Kenny!' He raised his hand in acknowledgement. 'STOP YOU BUGGER!' they cried. My dad looked up to see there was no ferry at the end of the steps. And this from a man who couldn't swim.

Only more recently have I looked back at my dad's journalism career and appreciated the similarities with my forays in music. He had several businesses on Mull, including the building firm, that had not worked out as he'd hoped. Really, he was doing all he could to stay on the island, with us, but the mainland was always calling. He had been a talented footballer. He was offered contracts with professional teams but declined them. He had been a talented athlete – he held the Tobermory Highland Games triple jump record for fifty years, and still holds some of the sprint records – but none of those opportunities could take him away.

Then, in his early thirties, he started making demo tapes, interviewing some of the great old-timers mulling around Tobermory. There was the aforementioned Big Al. There were Dykes and the silent Agnes – Agnes, who always walked twelve paces behind her husband Dykes, who wore a skipper's hat even on bar stools. And Pluto, Bobby Butter, Mrs Tosh, Dougie

Puck, Jimmy 'Bechty' – who walked in overalls in far-reaching strides with dignified silence – and many more. Some of these characters have also inspired my music and fiction. But my father got to them first. He interviewed them about their lives and what had changed on the island. He passed the tapes onto the bread van, which then ferried them from Mull to Inverness, where they were dropped off at BBC Highland. And within three to four years my father had become one of Scotland's foremost journalists.

He would always get the story. Every story. Whether it was happening on Mull, or on a national scale. He once hid in a broom cupboard in the Inverness hotel the then Prime Minister, Margaret Thatcher, was staying in, only to emerge, microphone in hand, to get the scoop. He would tell John Major he hoped England's cricket team would get stuffed, producing a cheeky grin, only to then get the story. I know these tales now, and I heard them then, but not from my father. He never really spoke to us about his work. He spoke to us about being a family unit. About remembering where we belonged.

But my father working away all week, and travelling so haphazardly, did have its effects on me. I was about seven when the bread van gave him his big BBC break and he had to start working away. I missed him dreadfully. But I never talked about it. Although I'm sure my parents could see.

I developed a system to help me cope. Every Monday morning at 6 a.m. as he prepared to leave, I would secretly get up in the dark to stand behind my bedroom door at the back of the house. I'd listen as he went through his breakfast routine. I could hear the pips of the *Today* programme on BBC Radio 4 crackling out from the kitchen. His throat clearing. I'd smell his burnt toast. But I'd stay out of view. Then, immediately after the radio was switched off and I heard the familiar thud of the front door closing, I would rush from my bedroom to the spare room opposite at the front of the house. From there I would stand back, just far enough out of view, and watch from the window as he performed the familiar reversed turn of whatever car it was he was driving at the time, the tail lights gradually disappearing into the early morning dusk. I would rush back to my bedroom then, touch various parts of the room's furniture – always the same sequence of touches – and close my eyes and pray that he would be safe. Pray that the door of whatever classroom I was in later that morning wouldn't be opened by the head teacher, or even worse my mother, to tell me my father had crashed. New Order's 'Blue Monday' on twelve-inch was my favourite record at the time, but the aptness of the title seemed to escape me.

One Monday morning in winter I was sure the front door hadn't closed. And the radio continued to blast away. I had stayed in bed and it was beginning to turn light outside. I was certain Dad must have fallen asleep in the kitchen. Meaning he would miss the ferry! My heart was pumping with anticipated joy. I tiptoed to the kitchen door and prodded it open. But he wasn't there. Only the smell of coffee and burnt toast lingered.

I have never considered myself a religious person – as I have already mentioned, my father allowed my brother and me to give up our Sunday school careers after just one week – but I would pray to God the exact same prayer every Monday morning, and then again on Thursday evening, on the eve of my father's return journey home. Always the same. For years. He had countless accidents, but nonetheless I seriously believed I was keeping my father alive with this series of private, strategically placed touches and memorised prayers. It was exhausting. And I never told anyone. And now, years later, I have, in a new song called

'14 Year Old Boy'. That was how I was beginning to say most things.

The happiest I felt around this time was when we had a week off school and would go off with Dad, accompanying him on his journey. On those Monday mornings I was relieved of my routine because I was going with him. The pips of the *Today* programme would crackle down the car radio somewhere on Ardnamurchan instead of in the kitchen, as sheep acting as rubber tyre bollards cowered in our wake. It was like a *real* roller coaster. An adventure! To the mainland. To guitar shops. Restaurants. Cinemas. And to the sound of John Peel's voice without the aid of a coat hanger.

Often on those exciting excursions to the rest of the world, we boys would be decamped outside a posh hotel room, only to see the wild mane of Michael Heseltine emerge with my father in tow; or we would be sat outside the house of an influential Trade Union leader in Lanarkshire. I once even got an autograph from Sheena Easton in the BBC studios. But I drew the line at resurrecting the horse dance.

Even now, with my father gone almost twenty years to his grand prix in the sky, a melancholy still hits me on Sunday. A feeling that I want Sundays to last for ever, or never to happen at all. So that nobody has to leave on Monday. My mum's Barbra Streisand *Guilty* album was the soundtrack to those nights, especially if Dad had had to leave early on the paper boat on a Sunday afternoon instead. We played scrabble to take my mind off it. And as time went on, and the vinyl spun, I did feel guilty, fearing it was my choice, my longing to stay, that was contributing to keeping us on the island, and therefore prolonging our separation. Maybe it was no accident that Dad died on a Sunday night too. But despite what I put myself through as a child, it is a source of comfort to me now that my dad pursued his passion as I suppose I have too. But, as with me, it was the island that made him.

MY OWN FIRST demo tapes were posted to London from the post office on Tobermory Main Street. I was in my late teens by then, and realising that, despite the 'X', not many record company executives were going to see my TRAX gigs in the Aros Hall, nor be visited by the bread van. I knew a record deal was about as likely as placing a demo tape in a one-legged seagull's mouth and telling it to fly to London.

Around this time my songwriting was becoming prolific. I was learning to play other instruments, hearing harmonies, creating basslines, and realising how they needed to sit in partnership with the lead vocal. I loved synthesised choirs, programming drums, and I now had a four-track recorder to go with my Fender telecaster to capture all this. At the same time, TRAX morphed into an edgier affair. A new band. We wore shades. We smoked cigars on stage. We rehearsed in the house belonging to the Tobermory Distillery, using broom handles as make-shift mic stands. We became the Love Sick Zombies (LSZ) and we played our first show in the hall in 1992. Our friend Marjorie so named us that summer after having to listen to us torturously cataloguing how the sweet-smelling daughters of these prosperous-looking Yachties (mainlanders in yachts) seemed to look right through us as they dined in Tobermory's seafront's restaurants, while we sat on the railings opposite with our tongues out.

The LSZ line-up was me on guitar, now singing too, Paul on drums (on a kit so polished that it blinded you if you looked at it), Gordy on bass and vocals, and Alan – maybe realising there wasn't much of a career to be had managing TRAX – now playing rhythm guitar and doing vocals too. MacInnes – grandson of 'Pibroch' and now one of Scotland's finest ceilidh drummers – we poached from Warnings Against Folly to add percussion on tracks like, 'Sympathy For the Devil'. The posters were distributed around the island. We were even old enough by then to apply for the bar licence ourselves. We decided to dress the hall in a way The Velvet Underground, U2 or Warnings

Against Folly would have done. And then the day arrived: our first gig.

Before we struck a note, we had to go through the elaborate ritual of putting the stage extension up. It wasn't exactly fit for a Freddy Mercury crowd-walk at Wembley Stadium, but the extra four foot did mean we would be able to puff cigar smoke closer to the audience. The erection of the stage was a ritual. But we were mere spectators. It involved going to a small man called Mat. Mat was Iris's husband, and janitor of the Aros Hall. He was in his late sixties but would insist on putting up the dozen or so heavy segments of the stage himself. I have never seen a Herculean act like it. And all this without a word uttered or a flake of cigarette ash dropped from the side of his mouth. We had nothing but respect for him, but we always tossed a coin to decide who had to be brave enough to knock on Mat's door.

With the stage set, we ran through a pre-show soundcheck. When we were happy with all the levels, we took a break and I popped my head out the door of the hall to see Dykes in his skipper's hat and Agnes sitting opposite in the shelters (a covered area that we used as a makeshift goalmouth, with toilets at either end). They were their usual distance apart.

Dykes reached out his long, thin finger and ushered me over. I walked across the road to him with my guitar still strung on my back in the way of Bruce Springsteen and The Edge. I got close enough to see Dykes' gums. And Agnes' weathered face. Both of them toothless masks. Just below us, Dykes' prized little wooden rowing boat was moored: named *Agnes*. There was something about how he had named his beloved rowing boat after this woman who he never seemed to speak to, and who he walked twelve paces in front of, that moved me (it would go on to inspire the boat named *Eliza* in *Ivor Punch*.) Dykes' big finger lured me even closer. He nodded towards the hall from where I'd come. I leant into him. 'What a racket,' he croaked.

I tried to put Dykes' critique out of my head and crossed the road back to the hall. I stopped to talk to one of the older girls I used to play tennis with, who had recently arrived home from university. She smiled and asked what time the show started. I might have uttered the words 'guest list' for the first time in my life. We never had a guest list. Or if we did, Dykes and Agnes certainly didn't want to be on it.

Soon it was time to put on the new purple jacket I'd commissioned big Scott Murray to make especially for the show. Scott was the father of our friend Keiran from Warnings Against Folly, and was also known on the island as 'Scott Fruit 'n Veg' because he had a fruit van. But in an earlier life he had been a tailor on Savile Row.

When we walked on stage at 11.30 p.m. the crowd had been kept waiting long enough. We were puffing on cigars like Bono's 'The Fly'. It wasn't the biggest crowd, but the show started off with a bang, and thankfully it wasn't the PA system. We went straight from 'Zoo Station' (which Gordy sang through a flanger guitar effects pedal) to 'Jackie Wilson Said' and from there to the Happy Mondays. There were some girls in the audience – and not all of them were my cousins. We wore attitude like bad cologne.

We even had our own 'Bez', who was the infamous Happy Mondays' side-of-stage dancer-in-chief, in the shape of a harmless bespeckled man who Dodo the painter had christened 'The Enterer'. The Enterer was in his late thirties (ancient) and looked more like an accountant than Bez. He had arrived on Mull that summer from the Midlands, twenty-five years too late, armed with lopping Flower Power dance moves and a bodhrán. He was a permanent presence, along with his instrument, at every party on the island that summer. And here he was accompanying us from the hall floor. I wasn't best pleased. There wasn't a bodhrán on 'Kinky Afro'. But at least he wasn't on the stage.

I spotted a shark hat crossing the floor. The hat dotted around, from cluster to cluster. This was it. My big moment. An A&R man from London had received the demo tape and gig flyer. He was wearing a long coat like they must do in London: Withnail-like. But he was short. And old. And he was a she . . . It was my grandmother. She had marched along the seafront at midnight to collect Iona, one of my visiting cousins, who at fifteen had broken the bank flat curfew.

We played a few more gigs that summer, including a messy impromptu affair in a tent at Calgary Beach as guests of Stretch Dawson. I even played drums for the first time on Jimi Hendrix's 'Hey Joe'. But the most significant moment for me was when I first introduced one of my own songs into the set. We were in the distillery house on the seafront, each of us playing the same song in a different room, imagining we were starring in our own distilled version of *A Hard Day's Night*. I'm not even sure the others noticed. It was thrilling to hear my music being played outside the confines of my bedroom, of my bubble. It was the song that would become 'Tobermory Zoo'. It wasn't a secret between me and the post office letter box any more, or between me and some list of faceless names in London; none of whom likely wore shark hats anyway. But they would hear about me. I was sure of that.

My musical education was all happening outside of school. In school we had a few broken glockenspiels and a white drum kit. Everyone could play the opening snare parts of ZZ Top's 'Gimme All Your Lovin'' and U2's 'Sunday Bloody Sunday'. But I preferred to discover music for myself. I knew I was making all kinds of mistakes (I only heard about 'concert pitch' after I'd already demoed about three hundred songs), but when I was making music, or sketching stage plans, or working out arrangements for my band, it was like living in a kind of golden time or in a starry sky. Music seemed to burn inside me. I liked art too, and had an inspiring and talented artist as my teacher, Mr Archbold, and I was also pretty decent at most sports, but nothing excited me like music. Like watching Live Aid. Or even the Mull Music Festival.

The Festival was a long way from T in the Park, Glastonbury, Reading, Leeds or the V Festival (all of which awaited me), and to this day it remains a traditional folk music festival rather than a rock one, but it was the most exciting thing, to have all these punters and musicians descending on our little town each spring. The Mishnish Hotel and the MacDonald Arms were the places to be.

I remember one year having my nose pressed against the outside window of the Mishnish's Galleon Grill. That was the bar named in honour of the sunken Spanish ship out in the bay. But it wasn't flamenco I was listening to. Rumour had it that the Eagles were in town. I was fairly certain even then that the Eagles didn't come from Oban, but it turned out there was a band called the Eagles from Oban who would be playing in the Mishnish that night. The only problem was I wasn't quite old enough to get in. I can still remember the tall man with bald head and beard, who looked like he would be more at home on the board game *Guess Who?* than with a Fender Telecaster strapped over his shoulder, singing 'Take It Easy', as if it had been written in Argyll. He *was* taking it easy. The whole band was, all the Oban Eagles. It looked effortless. I wanted one of those guitars. I wanted to be the tall man. I wanted whatever the mainland had. I was sick of waiting for their films, their music. I was sick of it taking my dad away five days a week.

Years later, I played my first MHS hometown gig at the Mull Music Festival: a two-night run in MacGochans (named after a long-gone local character). People from MTV were there, along with writers from music monthlies and others. People from my record label too: the legendary Geoff Travis from Rough Trade Records, who had signed The Smiths! My gran even ended up in *The Face* magazine. Now a gold disc for my debut album, *Loss*, hangs in that room in MacGochans. Twenty-four-carat dog in wig.

But I didn't know what the future had in store for me that night as I pressed my face to the window, glued to the Oban Eagles, my nose just about smelling the whisky and warm beer on the other side of the glass. I just knew I wanted to be on the inside.

FRIDAY NIGHTS WERE always joyous. On TV there was *Cagney & Lacey*, *Cheers* and *The Tube*. And – my father came home. But one Friday night, several days before Christmas, my father walked into the house and I'll never forget his ashen face. He basically walked in and out of the door in the same step. He never did that. It was because it had been a tragic week for my hometown: two days previous, the Lockerbie plane disaster had happened. That week, a world event, a global headline, washed up on our shores: the island lost one of its sons on the bombed plane. A talented golfer by the name of Willie McAllister. My father had been a local prodigy too, in sporting terms, and he had been a mentor of sorts to Willie. He was going straight down to be with Willie's uncle, Alec, who had brought up Willie and his younger brother.

In *The Letters of Ivor Punch*, I have fictionalised

something of how Lockerbie affected Mull. At times, I have wondered if I should have. In the book I even use the same seat number on the plane as Willie's. But it was written as a tribute to a good man, a star in the sky, and on an island too, that will never go out. The book is my attempt to capture a time, a place and a people.

I'll never forget how I watched my father driving off to comfort Willie's uncle that night. The sky and the sea looked like one thing, blacker than black. It was so dark we could have been part of the mainland. The whole town had a cloak thrown over it.

These events were not far from my mind fourteen years later, during my own maiden transatlantic flight – also to New York, only six months after another disastrous world event: 9/ll.

I was flying across my traced map of many years before. I was travelling to play my first MHS shows in the US. Three nights in NYC. I was also flying to the home of Pam, who was beside me and would soon become my wife. I remember feeling nervous about going there, but also extremely excited. Pam and her family were New Yorkers and I knew they were proud of their city, but I was also unsure of what to expect. During the flight I walked up the plane to stretch my legs. Unbeknown to me, I wandered into First Class. Micky Dolenz, the drummer from The Monkees, was standing alongside me wearing his big smile. He knew a thing or two about believing daydreams. Mine were all coming true. I was finally getting my own long-haul luggage tag.

We touched down and then travelled to be with Pam's family. I immediately felt, and still feel, very fortunate to have them in my life. Although I'd never been in America before, when I arrived in New York and received such a loving welcome from my new US family, it felt somehow like 'home'. And in the city, despite what it had so recently endured, I experienced such a strong sense of hope and resilience. It was like visiting a familiar place.

A year later, when Pam and I got married on Mull, my Palestinian-turned-American father-in-law, Elias Ghuneim, who became like a second father to me, met John Kirsop, my grandfather. They connected instantly, like long-lost brothers: a Bethlehem boy and a Muilleach. I think this was in part due to the fact that, in an almost unfathomable twist of fate, at the end of his army service in World War II, my grandfather had almost joined the Palestinian Army. But instead he had returned to Mull to take on the family plumbing business. Seeing them together, their immediate closeness, poking each other's pot bellies, proved to me that my instinct that *people are people* is true, and we can connect deeply and share our tales, wherever we come from.

Family greetings completed, on my first night on US soil, I had only one other place I wanted to be. I hailed a yellow cab to CBGB's. It was closing time and the last of the rockers were being asked to leave. Pam explained the extent of my journey and the doorman let us go inside to walk around. It was to be the first night of my love affair with that city, with America generally, and also with my new US family. This was the country that had given me so much. So much music, so many films and ice cream sodas. It had even made my Fender guitar. And now I was here. But the strange thing was, I felt more like the fourteen-year-old boy making music in my bedroom than ever before. I felt that I was doing what he wanted. I ended that night in the White Horse Tavern, where Dylan Thomas famously drank himself to death. In the *New York Post* on the bar there was an article with my face planted on it. As first bites of the Big Apple go, it wasn't a bad night. Then reality set in. As we walked home I saw the eerie, sad sight of two light beams up ahead escaping into the black Manhattan sky. A memorial. Twin Towers of light.

The first night of my series of gigs in New York arrived and there was a buzz in the air. Not because of me. Nor due to the fact that all the Love Sick Zombies were actually in the room. Two were even on the stage. (My friends had flown over for the shows, armed with kettle leads.) The electricity was of a different kind. It was because somebody even more unexpected was amongst us. Now I was really fourteen again. David Byrne from Talking Heads was in the room. I was introduced to him before I took to the stage. He told me he had been on the website and thought he would just show up. I tried to hear him over the music and so I asked him again, 'Sorry, *whose* website?'

'Yours,' he said.

MHS had recently performed alongside NYC band The Strokes on their electrifying debut tour of the UK, and he'd read about my music in connection with them.

'Thought I'd check it out,' he smiled, those goggle eyes fixing me.

As I walked to the stage to perform, the Statue of Liberty clearly visible through the venue windows, all I could think about were those evenings on Tobermory football pitch, listening to Byrne's voice booming out, and the nights I'd mimed his words into my hairbrush. I should have asked him about that snare drum. As I struck the first chords of 'Watching Xanadu', my first Top 40 hit, I wondered if John McEnroe or Björn Borg might show up next. Olivia Newton-John? Manhattan was just an island too, after all. Anything was possible.

And two years later my US love affair grew even further when I made my first album on US soil, in the town of Woodstock, upstate NY, where the famous festival had taken place thirty-five years previous, in the month following the moon landing. It was my third MHS album, *This is Hope*. I did feel hopeful. Obama was in the air. I was recording in the famous Bearsville Studios, which was still owned by the widow of Bob Dylan and The Band's famous manager, Albert Grossman. I recorded in the Turtle Creek barn studio there, where Dylan and The Band had recorded. Janis Joplin's Mini was still in the garage. Halfway into the recording, we lost an entire mix of a particularly fidgety arrangement for the song, 'This Is The Hebrides', when a power cut switched off the desk. It was like being back home. I almost ran for candles.

It was that evening I wrote the song 'Tree-scavengers' in reference to the flying turkeys all around the studios, but it was also about the men of Tobermory who would 'borrow' fir trees every Christmas from the local forestry supply. Ivor Punch does a bit of that too. And chirping away on the Bearsville fax machine were drawings from my cousin Julie, who was back on Mull and sending her impressions of the fifteen-foot papier-mâché dog with the wig we'd christen 'Trudy'. If my uncles had been Bob Dylan and Robbie Robertson, this is where they would have recorded too. That would have made Bob a plumber. I was OK with that. Especially when the water stopped working at the studios and I had to be driven to the local hotels for showers. Home wasn't so far away.

A week or so after I finished the album, Pam and I were in New York, walking around Soho one late afternoon. It was that time of day, the kind I love on Tobermory Main Street when the light gets a bit orange and the sea laps more gently to the shore. When the clock's chimes seem lazier. When Merrick used to think nothing of showing her big bra to the world. I looked up for her but of course there were only air-conditioning units and the Manhattan skyline looking down at me. It was stiflingly hot. It wasn't the windows of Tackle & Books I was looking into but a store called Penguin. I saw a hat I liked in a window. A kind of shark hat. Maybe I was trying to bring my grandparents to life. In any case, I went in and enquired about the hat. I wanted a medium size and they didn't have it. My wife nodded and smiled at me as I tried on the small. *Nah*, I thought. *Thanks anyway*.

We circled around Soho, grabbed a drink, visited MacDougal Street and the exact address where Bob Dylan first arrived in 1961. But then found ourselves back at the Penguin store. *Bugger it*, I thought. I went in and tried the hat on again. The girl in the store was laughing at this indecisive Scot. I played along.

I was paying for the hat at the till when I heard a song over the store's speakers. I knew that voice . . . It was my song – 'Don't Take Your Love Away From Me', from my second MHS album, *Us*. *Us* to signify family, as in shared community, as in what you need after *Loss*, as in, the US. It was a song I'd written for my wife. Here it was being played at my favourite time of day on another continent while I was buying a hat. That doesn't even happen to me on Tobermory Main Street. I still have the hat. And the wife. As we left the store, I realised I'd never felt so at home while being away. The teenager in me loomed large. Maybe this mainland isn't such a bad place after all.

And maybe this journey of musician to novelist, from islander to apparent mainlander, has been shorter than I imagined. The island is always closer than you realise. Wherever I am, I am always an islander. To paraphrase Bob Dylan in his excellent book, *Chronicles: Vol 1* – creativity comes from any form of motion, even just putting one foot in front of the other. And it must be the same riding waves. Leaving an island with dreams in your head will do that to you too. Because there is something about waves. How they repeatedly bring in the flotsam and jetsam of otherness, while at the same time reinforcing the familiar. Maybe that's where those dual states reside, at the shoreline: where islander meets mainlander. And it seems the process of writing is much the same as songwriting: the melodies and voices won't leave me alone. They go on making my past part of my future. Just as well. I still need that electric shock. I still need to plug in.

Mull is not mentioned in *The Letters of Ivor Punch*.

It is only referred to as 'The Island'. Why is that? It's hard to hide on a small island, so maybe it was a cop-out, in that I didn't want to offend anyone in the community. Or maybe I did it to signify the world *as* a community. I don't know. But I do know that people, their stories, and remembering those tales, is a big part of what keeps us alive. On my new – eighth – MHS album, *Wakelines*, I have that song '14 Year Old Boy'. I need to keep him close now. To feel the things he did. To make sure I don't let him, his hopes, his fears, his past, his dreams, go.

I was reminded a few years back – by an old Oban High School teacher of mine who turned up at an MHS New Year gig at Edinburgh Castle – that I had lugged a guitar and amp off the island before. Every week, in fact. My final two years of schooling were on the mainland, in Oban, and during the week us lads lived in a hostel. Every Monday morning I would bring my Fender Telecaster and amp on the first ferry to school. And I would carry them home again on Friday afternoons. I didn't mind; I couldn't be separated from them. There was also something comforting about emulating my dad's weekly travel routine. I could even see him on the Friday ferry, if he chose the correct gangplank. But around this time something happened to me: I fell ill in my final year. Really, I fell into an abyss.

I've never written about this before. I had never encountered symptoms like I was feeling that year. It was like the wrong kind of electric shock. I felt burned out. Fatigued. As though I wasn't there behind my eyes. I looked at friends and family and myself in the mirror and I felt like I didn't know anyone. I really did feel like the boy in the bubble. I panicked. I was convinced I was going crazy (it didn't help that we were studying schizophrenia in school), and so I decided to leave school one Tuesday afternoon. I dropped my studies and headed home on the last ferry on a wet, dark night in November 1988. A month before Lockerbie.

Everyone had university prospectuses – I myself was considering art school – but really all I wanted was to be Elvis, to be Bob Dylan, to be the Davids: Byrne and Bowie. But I felt more like one of Jackie Johnson's carcasses. My symptoms were making me more and more depressed and withdrawn. It was discovered I had immune system issues, possibly due to food intolerances. My diet in the hostel had been pretty terrible and I was showing some of the symptoms my mother had been suffering. I recovered slowly, over eighteen months, but during that time I thought I was losing myself. My mind. The only thing that kept me going was the music in my head. And learning to trust it. I began to realise they weren't voices. They were lyrics and melodies. I was a song-writer. Which wasn't to be found in the university prospectuses.

I sometimes think back to that day I left school with a fog in my head. I told Mr Morrison, my year tutor, that I was off to become a songwriter and I always remember he didn't laugh. He was a guitarist too. He tried to talk me out of it and then just smiled at me when he realised he couldn't, and said simply, '*Good luck, you'll need it*', as I walked out of his room of silent pupils. And then, thirteen years later, he was at my gig. I suppose dreams do come true. I had the Fender Telecaster with me on stage that night, and my Uncle John's old black and white bass too. Maybe my teacher could see into the future. Thankfully the fog cleared.

THESE HAVE BEEN just some of my hometown tales. The stories that continue to mean something, to mean something to me. And who knows, maybe they might even find a place on the shelves of Tackle & Books on Tobermory Main Street. Where I once passed with my first guitar in a blur of National Heath glasses. There are many more stories and I'm fortunate I have somewhere to put them. I'm lucky I have an audience, a community, to share them with. That's why we need tales: to bring people together, to understand how individual experiences become shared experiences. To belong. To leave a bit of us on the barbed-wire fence. So that those who come along to graze next know just a little of who we were. I hope my tales might make you think of your home. Think about where you belong. And how your home travels with you.

Me? I'll always lug an island with me. Plugged into the mainland.

I heard the New York author Paul Auster recently describing his writing process as being like trying to cast a net over lots of little details or observations. Well, mine were fished from the Atlantic Ocean. And this is my catch.

Taynuilt Safari
By Angus Macintyre
(*Northern Books from Famedram*)

There's the myrtle tang in the wild wind's breath
That blows from the Brander Pass
And the sweet perfume of the bonny broom
Gold-bright on the moorland grass.

And the only sounds to break the peace
That blesses my Highland hill
Are the whisper of the evening breeze
And a curlew's vibrant trill.

I pray I may hirple there once more
And rest by the singing stream
To watch on lone Loch Etive's shore
The wavelets froth and cream.

I yearn to recline on the lichened wall
I hurdled so oft in my prime
Perchance to hear the curlew's call
So sweet in my halcyon time.

Of course you'll come with me my Queen
For old men risk a fall
And I'll have your shoulder whereon to lean
Till we reach that lichened wall.

And we'll rest thereon in the gath'ring light
Till the fall of the daybreak dew
And the Taynuilt windows have cast their light
On Argyll's most wondrous view.

Should the kind Lord grant this old man's prayer
In the goodness of his will
My preview of paradise has been there
In the heavenly peace of the hill.

A9

Ellen MacAskill

ELLEN MACASKILL writes fiction and poetry. She graduated from the University of Glasgow in 2016. She is working on her first novel while living in Montreal.

For KT

1. COMING

ON THE TRAIN going north through Perthshire I realise I haven't cried yet, that I'm doing well compared to usual. My cheap coffee from the trolley spills onto the table in front of me and I soak it up with the sports section of the newspaper. The leaves outside are aflame with autumn colours, signalling the impending darkness. The afternoon train means getting distracted by this view, instead of staring at my own reflection gazing back at me from a black window. I've scribbled half a poem on the back of a receipt. I scrunch it up and tuck it into the bin behind my chair. Public transport poems never seem good enough by the time I reach my destination.

I check my phone:

*Let me know what time you get in. Me and the
cat are looking forward to seeing you! I've got in
some bread and things for tea. x x x Mum*

Last night's leaving party in Glasgow hangs over
me like a layer of smog, clogging up my senses
and making me nauseous. Food and quiet drinks
with friends at the vegan pub escalated into shots at
Sleazy's, then an hour dancing to chart music in the
biggest gay club in the Merchant City, then finishing
a year's worth of dregs of alcohol from my kitchen.
The last pals standing stayed until 7 a.m., when we
climbed to the top of the shaky scaffolding surrounding my Partick flat to look out on the city as the sun
rose. I didn't feel emotional about the goodbyes.
Maybe I'm in denial.

A book of feminist theory sits unopened on my
lap, one of the books I selected to get me through this
upheaval. Optimistically, I left most of my boxes of
things with various friends in Glasgow, so in theory I
could move back next week. My bank balance thinks
otherwise. Lots of people move home at this point
in life, I tell myself again as we hurtle through the
farmland of Scotland. No good jobs anywhere. Better
to spend time with family for a while than work long

hours in the city just to pay rent. We all have to do it these days. Nothing is permanent. I mouth the phrase again and again to myself like a mantra — *nothing is permanent nothing is permanent* — as we pass through Aviemore and my hands twitch for nicotine.

'The next stop is Inverness, where this train will terminate.'

2. INVERNESS, 2007

I FIRST MEET Kathy in drama club at the beginning
of secondary school, after she moves to Inverness from
Wick. The drama department provides a safe haven for
weirdos and cooler kids to mix, and a fertile ground for
my crushes on older girls. I don't call them that at this
point – crushes are reserved for messy-haired boys who
spend all day in the music room – but I'm infatuated
with these girls, a rotating cast of sixteen-year-olds
with clothes too edgy for the Highlands. I try my best
both to be like them and to make them notice me.

In second year, I act a small speaking part in
Macbeth, the Porter, who appears for one scene only.
We rehearse this scene three times as a group, so for
the rest of the after-school rehearsals that winter I sit
on the sidelines giving prompts to Lady Macbeth, or
raid the props cupboard with the funny, flamboyant
boy who plays the Doctor.

Kathy sweeps into rehearsals and instantly trans-fixes me with her mature aura. She dresses like a goth, the perfect Weird Sister #1, dyed jet-black hair and fishnet tights under long skirts, pop-punk band T-shirts and studs all up her ears. She spends breaks between scenes giggling with the girls playing Weird Sisters #2 and #3, and sometimes I overhear them talking about who was the most drunk at the party in the woods last weekend, or who has a free house this weekend. But even though she chats with the other girls in drama, they never hang out together at lunch. I often see Kathy smoking by the trees outside the gate with the stoner boys, or sitting on her own reading behind the geography huts. I hear she plays bass in a band with Emma, that tomboyish girl who always looks angry, but I haven't heard them play.

She's tall for fifteen, with a Western Isles accent inherited from her dad who comes from Lewis. My mum hears from someone else's mum that she lives with her dad and older brother, Jack. Her mum came to Scotland from Poland but died when Kathy was wee. I start practising my eyeliner to make it look like Kathy's, with flicks at the end and blue mascara. I see on her Bebo page that she likes Paramore so I buy their album and listen to it on repeat all month.

One day in the week before the show, the girl playing Weird Sister #3 misses rehearsal, but Ms Mackie wants to run the scene anyway. I offer to fill her spot, barely needing the script handed to me. Kathy smiles at me as I step on stage. I immediately get self-conscious about the sweat under my arms, a chronic problem at thirteen. Despite my black T-shirt, during the spell I worry about lifting up my arms when we join hands in a circle in case anyone in the audience sees the patches from there. My hand in Kathy's ('*The weird sisters, hand in hand, posters of the sea and land*') feels clammy. I hear someone snigger in the audience when Macbeth enters and I freeze up and turn red under the hot stage lights, convinced I'm the object of their amusement. But I manage to speak my lines to Macbeth and Banquo and scurry off, cackling, to the wings with Kathy and Weird Sister #2.

'Well done! Thanks for stepping in,' says Kathy as soon as we get out to the hallway. Weird Sister #2 paces up and down the corridor, repeating '*Not so happy, yet much happier*' under her breath, after forgetting the line for a long painful moment onstage.

'No bother!' I say breathlessly.

'You're good in the Porter scene by the way, Alice. It's a really good wee monologue when someone plays it well,' she says, taking the pins out of her bird's nest of hair so it falls down around her shoulders.

'Thanks! So you've seen *Macbeth* before?'

'Oh yeah, it's my favourite Shakespeare. I've watched some adaptations but try not to mimic any one version too much.'

'Cool,' I say. The only other Shakespeare I know is the one with Leo DiCaprio. 'I think my mum taped one off the BBC recently.'

'I can lend you the DVD of my favourite film of it to watch it before the show,' Kathy says, leading the way back into the theatre.

'That'd be great!' I whisper as we sneak back towards our seats, while Ms Mackie tries to control some boys forgetting the no-contact rule of stage combat.

Over the years, we become drama friends. Outside of the rehearsal rooms we don't talk much, just smile and wave to each other in the corridors, but she becomes less and less intimidating, and I start to think she likes hanging out with me. She moves to Edinburgh to do a college course in social work when I'm in fifth year and we lose touch for a while.

The summer after, when I've just left school, we bump into each other at RockNess music festival.

After kissing a clingy boy in the dance tent, I'm wandering the campsite avoiding him when she calls me over to her pitch near the muddy path. Her hair is shorter now, with purple streaks, and floral tattoos decorate her left arm, but I recognise her instantly. Sitting together in camp chairs, drunk in the afternoon, she tells me how she's here with her girlfriend from Edinburgh, but they had an argument and she stormed off. I share my menthol cigarettes and rum from the hip flask in my bra.

She asks me about school and if I'm going to uni. She tells me about her girlfriend, Sid, how they moved in together last month and she loves her but they bicker when Sid gets too drunk. Sid's older than Kathy and works the door at one of the gay bars in Edinburgh. Kathy tells me she's so busy with coursework and her placement that she doesn't go out much. I listen in awe. I've never had a lesbian friend before. In the photos Kathy shows me on her phone, Sid reminds me of Emma from her band in school – tall, with barely-there bleached blonde hair and boyish clothes.

When it starts to rain we take shelter in her tent. When I find my friends later they all ask what I've been doing in a tent with the lesbian from Wick.

3. INVERNESS, 2016

I ENTER THE rural pub near my mum's house at five on a Tuesday, lingering in the doorway with my hood dripping into a puddle around me. The same regulars as always prop up the bar and turn to look at me when they hear the door. No sign of her yet. The small room smells of old beer and dust, the TV plays football highlights beside the unused dartboard, and a shiny new jukebox with a touchscreen sits by the opposite wall. I go to the bathroom, the women's stalls clean from lack of use. I look at myself in the mirror – short dyed-red hair messy as usual, no lipstick or food on teeth, no marks on T-shirt – and reflect on the nerves hanging ominously in my chest. Not as if this is a date. We're just two old school friends back in our hometown meeting for a casual drink.

Back out in the bar, I sit down at a table by the window and take out my phone. Before this week, we last sent messages to each other two years ago. We didn't keep in contact much, but I always hoped to see her over the holidays.

Kathy: *Hey! Are you at home for Hogmanay? Let me know if you're in town, it'd be great to catch up x*

Alice: *Hey, how's it going? Sorry, I'm heading back to Glasgow tonight to work. Annoyed we missed each other again! Let me know next time you're here and we can get a drink x*

Kathy: *I rarely make it away from Edinburgh these days but will let you know if I'm ever west! Happy new year when it comes xx*

'Alice!'

I look up to see her standing beside me.

'Kathy! Hi. Did you walk here?' I ask, taking in her black and blue hair stuck wet to her collar.

'Got the bus that stops in Balloch,' she says, wringing her hair. Her Western Isles accent lilts like a song, like it used to. 'I forgot how long it takes to walk from there. Sorry I'm late. Can I get you a drink?'

'Tennent's would be lovely!' I say. Wow, I think,

who describes Tennent's as lovely? But it's too late to make a joke now that she's dumped her leather jacket on the seat and gone to the bar. I watch her, clocking the full-colour tattoos curling around her arms and the lick of skin between her T-shirt and belt. Nick the Barman, who has seen me in too many states, smiles as he serves her.

Sitting a glass down in front of me, Kathy asks, 'So, how have you been?'

'Cheers for this,' I smile, and we clink pints. 'Yeah, it's been a while . . . I don't know where to start.'

'When did you get back to Inverness?'

'Just about a week ago,' I say. 'You've been here since summer?'

She nods into her pint. 'Yeah, my work contract in Edinburgh ended in June and they had no funding to give me good hours, so I came back to save. I've picked up shifts as a carer in sheltered housing, but I worked with disabled youth before, so I'm looking to get back into that.'

Her job directly helps people! Amazing, I think.

'That's good,' I say. 'And how do you find living at home?'

'Oh, you know . . . okay. Not many friends around though. None, actually,' she laughs sheepishly.

'Is Jack doing all right?' I have never spoken to Kathy's brother but it seems polite to ask. He was older and good at sports in school. One of the lads.

'He's fine, yeah. Junior doctor in Manchester, he stayed there after finishing medicine. Doesn't come up north much, no time.'

'So just you and your dad.'

'Yeah,' she says. 'It's a bit different now. I think he has dementia. His short-term memory has gone to shit and he's got no one to help with day-to-day stuff, so that's one of the reasons I'm still here. When I was away I'd call him every week, and it'd be easy to pretend not to notice it. Then I got back and it was worse than I thought.'

'I'm sorry,' I say.

'It's not your fault,' she says, shaking her head. 'It's fine. It's mostly cleaning and appointments and bills he needs help with. He's still good chat.'

'Good.' Not sure how to change the subject, I ask, 'Do you smoke?'

'I quit three months ago, but sure. Can I bum a fag off you?'

Under the corrugated iron shelter outside, we give each other a rundown of the minimal details of our adult lives so far, the flats we've lived in and jobs we've had, the school friends we've seen and those we've avoided, brushing over the hard parts – the heartbreaks, the fear, the debts – with nervous laughter. We discuss all the people from our school who have also come out since leaving. She laughs when I realise that more than one of the boys I fancied back then turned out to be gay. I buy more pints and we put songs on the new jukebox. She picks a Lauryn Hill classic, and I follow it with 'You Oughta Know' by Alanis Morisette to annoy the old men.

'Do you ever play in bands any more?' I ask when we go out to smoke again, thinking back to Kathy playing a shiny red bass guitar in the school concerts, later ascending with a pop-punk band of outcasts to the tiny new music stages at the local festivals. In my memory, she looks intense and moody standing behind that bass, wearing a baseball cap unironically.

'Nah. Things didn't end very well with the band. Emma got pissed off at something and pulled out of the last show we were supposed to play together without telling us, and ... anyway, it's old news now. I like playing guitar alone still.' She applies some cocoa butter lip balm from a tin. 'What about you, do you still write poems? You were good at that. I totally stalked your blog back in the day.'

'Oh god,' I say, taking my turn to get nervous and laugh. 'Yeah, I mostly write fiction now instead of poems . . . well, I write poems when I'm drunk and sad but no one sees them.'

'I would love to read your drunk sad poems!' she says. 'That's my favourite genre.'

When she leans in to light my cigarette it occurs to me that I want to kiss her, but in my peripheral vision I can see the men sitting inside, some staring, and remember why gay kids from here usually move south. They get tired of sticking out.

Through the window, I spot a figure entering the room through the front doors. As soon as I clock him, my throat tightens and I feel sick. He strolls up to a table in the middle of the room and greets the man sitting there with a pat on the back, his ashy blond hair spiked with gel and acne scars on his cheeks. I take a small step back, out of view of the window. My breath quickens until I feel I might stop breathing altogether.

'Are you all right?' she asks, following my line of sight in through the window, where Andy sits grinning with his friend.

'Can we go?' I say, my voice tiny.

Kathy nods and follows as I grab my bag and walk

quickly out of the side exit from the smoking area, around the car park and onto the single-track road by the pub. It's dark and the rain has left everything misty and damp.

'Sorry – sorry about that,' I stammer as I stop and turn to face her.

Her concerned eyes find mine and leave me exposed. 'Do you want to talk about it?'

I cover my eyes with my hands and sigh, 'Sorry – it's just that guy who just walked in there – I can't deal with him, I can't be around him.'

'That's okay. It's okay, Alice,' she says. Car headlights appear around the corner of the nearby crossroads and she takes my arm and pulls me away to the side of the road. We stop between the concrete and the ditch lining the adjacent field, waiting for the traffic to pass. Her arm reaches behind my back, around my waist, and I want to relax into it but I'm jittery with panic. 'Do you want me to walk you home? We can talk about it another time if you want.'

I nod and clench my jaw, mortified by the whole scene. Why did I have to do this in front of Kathy? Why did he have to turn up now? He probably wouldn't even recognise me.

We walk in silence down the dark road towards

my mum's house, her hand on my back guiding me, holding me up. She doesn't invite herself in when we reach the door, just hugs me, kisses me on the cheek, then turns out into the night to walk back to the bus stop alone.

4. INVERNESS, 2012

'**ALICE, COME TO** the toilets!' Molly beckons me from across the pool table.

'All right, coming – take my turn for me, Andy!' I pass him the cue and skip after her.

In the empty girls' toilets, Molly takes out a bag of drugs from her bra. She has the best cleavage in Culloden.

'You got a fiver?' she asks.

I search my purse and find a crumpled Bank of Scotland note for her to roll up.

'Should we do it in the cubicle?' I ask, glancing at the door.

'Nah, there's no other girls here who'd care,' she says, cutting up small lines with her cousin's ID. Nick the Barman hasn't asked us for ID once since we started drinking here six months ago, but we play it safe and bring fakes with us in case.

'Is it coke?'

'Yeah, Danny got it for me.' I haven't done coke before, but I know Molly has, at that festival we went to this summer, so I brace myself to join her. I can't let her get high without me. I blow my nose in preparation as Molly sniffs two lines, then I take the fiver from her, stick it up my nose and angle it to the white powder. The stuff hits the lining of my nostrils like inhaling nail varnish remover and I sniff a couple of times.

'Watch out!' scolds Molly when my cuff brushes close to the last line on the counter by the sink.

'Oh, sorry,' I say. 'Maybe I'll just have one for now.'

'Go on, Alice, I cut that one for you. I'll be flying if I take it!'

'Fine,' I say, and snort the remaining drugs, then wipe away the residue with some loo roll.

'Woo!' she yells, looking at us in the mirror side by side and turning round to kiss me on the cheek. Her highlighted curls tumble down into my long red hair between our shoulders. She's taller than me in her heels, a tight orange skirt peeking out under her leather jacket. She tried to make me wear her body-con black dress earlier, but I defected back to my ripped jeans at the last minute, along with a sports bra under my checked shirt, worn unbuttoned to expose a couple of inches of midriff. I mostly fold my arms to cover it.

Molly reapplies her pink lip gloss, then struts back out to the bar with me at her heel. She goes straight up to where Danny stands, kisses him in front of everyone, and I watch, confused by her attraction to this twenty-six-year-old waster.

'Alice! It's your fucking turn, eh! We're waiting on you!' Andy calls me over to the pool table. I march up to him, grab the pool cue from his hand and gesture like I'm going to whack it in his face. He flinches so hard that I burst out laughing and turn around to take my shot. I miss the yellow ball, pot the white, dump the cue on the table while Andy laughs at me, then go to the bar. The coke has given me a fucking invincible feeling, so I order a tequila and a pint to maintain it.

'Alice, I think Andy's into you, eh,' slurs Danny, hanging off Molly's shoulder. She gazes up at his stubble and giggles.

'Nah, you can tell him I'm all right, thanks. Not my type really.'

'So I've heard,' sniggers Danny. Molly buries her face in his arm.

'What?' I say.

'Nothing! I didn't say anything, Alice, take a chill pill!' he says.

Lesbianlesbianlesbian, I hear. Maybe I should fuck him just to prove them wrong, coke-brain thinks. But I'm seventeen and still not ready.

I throw back a shot of tequila and keep my face totally composed in that practised way despite the taste, then grab my beer and go to the jukebox. I put on Rihanna to piss off Danny, followed by 'Breed' by Nirvana and 'Sandstorm' by Darude. My heart has come loose and bounces around my chest and I can't stop focusing on my breathing, like if I don't I might just forget to inhale and exhale, inhale, exhale. I grit my teeth and stare around the small room until Molly comes over to talk to me.

'How are you feeling?' she asks, putting her arm around me in a flourish of Dolce and Gabbana perfume.

'Pretty fucking high, Molly,' I say, then continue before I can stop myself. 'You know, I wish Danny wouldn't make comments like he did before, about me being gay or whatever, and like when he was calling Andy a poof earlier, I could just tell he was doing it to piss me off because I had a go at him about it last week, and he was looking at me when he did it, and I'm sorry, Molly, 'cause I know you like him and everything, but Danny can be a lot of work some-times—'

'Don't take it personally, Alice, it's just banter, they don't mean it, they're cool with gay people, that's just how they tease each other, you know what I mean? And I want you and Danny to get along 'cause you're one of my best pals and I really like Danny, I think I love him and it'd be shite if you didn't like each other 'cause I want you to hang out with us! You're one of my oldest friends, Alice, and I'm gonna fucking miss you when you move, and want to see you while I still can! You'll forget me when you go to uni and make smarter pals!'

'Och, Molly, you know we'll stay pals, I love you too much to not come home and visit, and you can visit me all the time! The clubs are way better in Glasgow and we'll be eighteen by then so there'll be no stopping us! I just wish the boys would have some sensitivity, I hate people thinking they can walk all over me, you know?'

The last-orders bell rings for the second time and Molly jumps, retracting her arm from its place around my neck. The pub has emptied out, I realise, looking around at the stools up on the tables and the empty glasses on the bar. I wait for the question.

'Alice,' Molly says. Here it comes. 'Is your mum around tonight?'

'No,' I say. Molly knows my mum likes to gallivant at weekends. 'She's visiting my uncle in Edinburgh.'

'Do you think we could go back to yours? You're not in work tomorrow are you?'

'I'm off tomorrow,' I say, looking around at Danny and Andy trying to talk Nick the Barman into selling them a carry-out of beer.

'Let's go back for a bit! The boys promise they won't make a mess!'

Usually at this point I'd try to think up an excuse, but I'm too wired to go home on my own right now, and we're banned from Molly's house since we broke the sink in her mum's en suite bathroom two weeks ago and I still haven't written that apology note about it.

I leave the pub ahead of the others to nip home and clear up the living room, hide my mum's vodka from view, put away the underwear drying on the rack. I am giving myself a pep talk in the mirror as they knock a couple of times on the door and then tumble in – Molly, Danny, Andy. They carry bags full of Tennent's cans and stink of smoke.

'Remember to hide the cigarette butts if you're going to smoke on the patio, yeah?' I say feebly as the music gets turned up and my best friend and two strange boys explode into the tiny living room of my home. More lines of coke are cut and snorted off the coffee table. Andy switches on the TV to look for the football results, but Molly drowns it out playing music at full blast on the hi-fi. Soon Danny has picked up my acoustic guitar and plays along with the three-chord songs at an obnoxious volume. I scurry about with a can in one hand, going to check on the cat hiding in my mum's room every ten minutes or so, burying my face in her soft black fur and whispering, *I'm sorry, it'll be all right, don't be stressed*. Poor Moss. Petrified.

I go outside to the back garden to smoke a cigarette and find Andy already standing there.

'Nice stars!' I say, spinning around in the cool air under the speckled navy sky.

'Aye, they're nice up here, eh, where there's no street lights or that.'

He looks younger in the gloom.

'Here, thanks for letting us come back, Alice.'

'No worries, man. Takes the heat off Molly to not be at her house for once.'

There's a pause as we smoke, blowing clouds into the summer night, me wandering around the patio and onto the grass, my bare feet cold.

'Alice,' Andy says from behind me. 'Is it true you and that goth girl shagged in her tent at RockNess this year?'

My cheeks burn. 'Fuck off, why would you ask that?'

'Och, I'm just curious! I've got no problem if you're a lesbian, it's just a bit of fun! And to be honest—'

The kitchen door opens, interrupting him, and Danny falls out followed by Molly. Things seem tense. Danny slurs, 'We're heading off Alice, but cheers as always for a class after-party, see you soon—'

'Oh,' I say, 'wait, Molly, can I talk to you?'

She doesn't catch my eye, just frowns and turns away, tugging at Danny's hand. 'Sorry, Alice, we have to go, I'll text you tomorrow though, yeah? I'll drive us to Burger King.'

I try to protest, but they push through the gate, barely waving goodbye, off out into the dark country roads to continue their argument alone. Everything is empty and quiet and odd all of a sudden. My body aches and I really need to shit.

'Back in a sec,' I say to Andy.

When I emerge from the bathroom, he hasn't left like I hoped he would.

'Are you gonna get home all right?' I ask.

He looks up and smirks. 'It'd take me for ever to walk. Next bus is in about two hours.'

'Right,' I say. 'You could use the phone, call a taxi.' It's so quiet in the house now at that pre-dawn point of greatest darkness and deepest silence. I take in the room – beer cans, cups, crisp crumbs, random clutter strewn about the floor and wet patches in the carpet.

'Or I could just hang out here for a bit. We could watch a film or something if you want?'

Half an hour later, in my single bed, with the laptop, we watch the opening scenes of *The Shining*. Hazy from tiredness but sobering up, I'm aware of the bits of Andy's body pressing on mine, his heavy head leaning on my shoulder. He smells of booze. The scenes flit past my vision – the big house, the men, the corridors – and I nod off, my head bouncing up from my chest and hitting the wall behind.

'Alice! Don't fall asleep on me!'

'Mm,' I mumble. He closes the laptop and pushes it to the bottom of the bed.

'Here,' he says, curling his body around mine and nudging me downwards. 'Let's just nap for a bit.'

I'm too tired to care when he puts his arm around my waist. My eyes are closed by the time his hand creeps up my shirt, around my body, then under my sports bra. I lie still, then roll a few inches away from him, eyes tight shut. A second later his hand moves back to its place on my chest, then his other hand is in my pants. My body freezes in the foetal position. His fingers push into me, getting more forceful every time I try to pull away. I'm wide awake from the feeling of my heart hammering inside my chest, his face over mine, coming towards my neck. I feel the nip of his teeth on my skin. Flight mode kicks in.

'Get off!' I eventually say, and roll off the edge of the tiny bed onto the carpet, then pick myself up in a rush. I look down at him half-naked on the bed, between the pink duvet covers I've used since I was twelve.

'Come on, Alice,' he says.

'Andy, get out! Get out of my bed!' I realise I'm laughing despite myself.

He doesn't move, just protests and gets defensive,

so I repeat myself until finally he crawls out of my bed and follows me to the living room.

'You can leave now,' I say.

'We should get to know each other better, Alice. I really like you.'

'Please leave,' I stand by the kitchen door, arms folded.

'I'm going, I'm going! Just let me get my jacket.' He makes a show of searching the whole room. I pick it up from the armchair and thrust it at him, still laughing, finding a joke somewhere.

'Goodnight kiss?' he says, finally stepping out of the door. I lean in to kiss him – who knows why – it seems stupid, imagining for a second that I want him to be there and to like me. He grins at me when I pull away, then wanders off into the early hours, leaving the gate swinging behind him. The cat comes into the kitchen and meows for food.

'Moss, it's too early for breakfast.'

I pick her up despite her protests and close the door, leaning my back against it and closing my eyes on the mess of the house facing me, breathing in her soft smell and focusing on the pounding in my head.

In the time it takes the sun to rise, I sit over the toilet bowl trying to make myself vomit; avoid my bedroom; collect all the rubbish in a bin bag, including the cigarette butts from the patio, and stuff it underneath the other rubbish in the bin outside; shower and exfoliate three times; pull out the sofa bed in the living room and pass out there with the cat purring on my chest as the morning sun streams in.

5. INVERNESS, 2016

IN LATE OCTOBER, I land a job for new graduates in the press office of the regional council. The whole headquarters visibly wasting away from budget cuts, I drop off newspaper clippings in offices, write press releases on behalf of officials, and ignore emails I don't understand.

'It's good for diversity for them to hire people like you,' my mum said when she told me to apply for it, quickly checking herself and adding, '– young people.'

This is the first time I've got paid for something other than serving coffee, so I feel good about it in the beginning, despite the grim grey office building and the rush-hour car shares with my mum, soundtracked by the out-of-date playlist of the local radio station. Working in the same building as her feels like an intrusion on her routine, but we never bump into each other during work days. She's holed up working hard in the HR department in a different building.

I try to make office work glamorous. I buy trousers and a pencil skirt. I pack salads for lunch, and take my own mug and coffee into the dingy kitchen on our floor. Not many people talk to me in there. I share a small office with the press manager, Dave, who seems bewildered by my presence in his space. He's been here twenty years, he often reminds me, and they'll cut his job over his dead body! Dave's protectiveness over all Highland Council-related media makes him reluctant to delegate tasks to me, an assistant he didn't ask for, but he lets me take over the Twitter account, admitting that 'the social networking websites' are not his thing. Otherwise, I find I can do minimal work and still get paid at the end of the month.

One slow morning, alone in the office, I am browsing Facebook over my third cup of coffee of the day, and notice a post from an old friend, Quinn, an exchange student I met at a queer book group in Glasgow two years ago. Quinn wrote performance poetry about racial micro-aggressions and reclaiming joy. Quinn had this earnest way of talking as if they cared deeply about all of my feelings and wanted to communicate all of their feelings in return, even in our first conversation. It made me suspicious until I realised they weren't faking. Maybe people in North America don't brush off emotions with self-deprecating jokes. After charming everyone in our scene for a year, Quinn flew back to Canada to finish their gender studies degree, leaving a trail of wistful, admiring nerds in their wake.

QUINN STARR is looking for a new home:
Moving from Vancouver to Toronto in the New Year, hit me up if you know of any cheap safe housing opportunities for a brown trans kid and their cat! xoxo

Good for Quinn, I think, clicking onto their profile and seeing pictures of them at parties covered in glitter, mixed in with dramatic shots of sunsets over mountains and urban beaches. What a life. Then I click on the home screen and scroll down the page to other pictures and articles and life moments, forgetting about Quinn once again.

Later, on my lunch break, I sit in the canteen alone eating soup. An old magazine on top of the pile by my table catches my eye. *SEE CANADA* shouts the headline of the advertisement on the back cover, red text emblazoned over a collage of photos of snowy landscapes and lakes and sci-fi cities lit up at night. When I get back to my desk, I look up flight costs out of curiosity. I start to sweat a wee bit as new possibilities ping up with every click, and soon I am on the Canadian immigration page.

The idea catches. Without big rent costs, I can save a bit of my pay cheque every month. I pore over online forums about work visas all week but don't mention it to anyone, except from sending a tentative message to Quinn. They tell me they've found a punk house to move into in Toronto and would be happy to help me find housing if I moved. I check average weather graphs for each city. I research Canadian novelists and musicians I assumed were American. I look at Google Maps, marvelling at the size of the place, reminding myself of the world beyond the Highlands.

I don't mention Canada to Kathy. After the first time we met up, we started to spend more time together, getting to know the adult versions of each other, as friends first, until, without addressing it, we slipped into a pattern of sleeping together, finally able to live out the relationship we wanted as teenagers. It's unlike any romance I've had – not like Glasgow, where everyone in the queer community had a long, entangled history of dating each other and each other's exes. My relationship with Kathy exists in a social vacuum. For years, I've actively avoided committing to anyone, kept all dates at arm's length. All my flings have been cut short by circumstance, or my fear of sex, despite my attraction to people of any and all genders. With Kathy it happens by accident.

We pass from one week in this town to the next, holding each other up and reminding each other we're still alive, that maybe some happiness is possible here for jaded girls like us. We coordinate our lunch breaks to meet in high-street coffee shops and bitch about work. We curl up in our childhood bedrooms at weekends and watch *Planet Earth* and all the best films in the Gay & Lesbian section of Netflix, then all the worst ones after that. She occasionally plays guitar for me. I don't see other friends often, just her and my workmates and my parents.

I don't really know how to be someone's girlfriend, and go from date to date hoping I'm making the right moves. I suppose relationships require sacrifice, but I can't temper my only-child selfishness. When I'm too sad to get out of bed, I flake on nights at her place at the last minute. I don't go to her with my feelings even when she encourages me, because that would mean facing up to them myself. I start to think relationships are friendships with added sex. Either way, I know Kathy is a babe. We both need something to temper the loneliness, as the nights draw in and the solstice beckons from the cold winter shadows.

6. GLASGOW, 2013

AT SEVENTEEN, I move to Glasgow to study philosophy and politics. Before leaving, I itch with restlessness, sick of gossip in Inverness accents and underage drinking, confused about the incident with Andy and my own body and desires. I leave and resolve to never move back long-term.

Almost a year passes. I reluctantly return for summer to save money by working at my old café job before moving into my new Glasgow flat. I'm recovering from baldness, after a friend shaved my head during study leave in second term. My ears and nose show off several more piercings than before, and my backpack is covered in badges ('Vote Yes!' 'Sex work is real work!' 'ACAB!'). Everything radical I've discovered down south bounces around my head, all of it so much bigger than me, and yet I feel compelled to show it off in arguments and call out all oppressive bullshit when I see it. A list of identities rolls around my tongue, ready to be reeled off at any moment. After much thought at feminist society meetings, Political Philosophy 1A, and 3 a.m. talks over Tesco Value red wine, I can now state that I, Alice from Inverness, am a *queer white bisexual feminist Leo pro-Scottish-Independence anarchist anti-racist assault-survivor poet who hates cops and Tories* (especially the ones from private schools in Edinburgh who interrupt me in tutorials). Any questions, refer to my blog.

These opinions make it difficult for me to interact with anyone from the 'straight world', which is a shame for my mum. She has long been my steady rock in this world: an unconditional carer, a best friend throughout our weird home life since Dad left, a social butterfly, and a cheerleader for my creative endeavours. Although younger than most of my friends' parents, she is also a well-meaning defender of gender roles who reads right-wing newspapers. She spends more time on the phone to her friends, planning their next weekend away, than thinking about the great inequalities in the world. We deal with the gay thing through a wordless agreement of 'don't ask, don't tell'. I can tell she wishes she could still dress me up cute and feminine and normal, like she used to. Watching the news together becomes a risky game. Certain topics of conversation get ruled out, unless I'm really in the mood for a fight: immigration, transgender people, fatphobia. When it gets too much, I stick my head in a book with a provocative title and sit sulking in the armchair.

Soon after I arrive back, Molly invites me out to the pub in town, Foxes. I stand with her and some other girls from school, listening to them gossip about boys they've met in Aberdeen, physically tensing to avoid the touch of sleazy men. It pains me to hear about the mediocrity straight women will accept from men in the guise of love. Losing interest, I shuffle outside to smoke. I look around, amazed that people wear high heels here, remembering the pain from when I used to wear them too. None of my new friends wear heels, except the ones who perform in drag. I find a dark corner and rock back and forth on my scuffed Doc Martens, scowling at no one in particular. I hope my battered leather jacket, held together by safety pins, worn over my baggy ripped jeans and T-shirt, gives off an illusion of toughness.

Then a voice walking by on the street says, 'Look, Kirsty. Check out the lesbian, eh. Thinks she's hard, doesn't she?'

'Hah, I thought that was a boy!'

'Nah, just a dyke I reckon.'

I tune into the voice and realise they're referring to me. When I look up, Kirsty laughs and sneers, 'You just need a good dick, gal! Sort you right out!'

The teenage couple disappear, giggling, off into the dark. I've been clocked. The familiar sensations provoked by catcalling fill my body, the rage and the comebacks that occur to me after the catcaller has left the scene. But these comments ring differently in my ears than sexual advances did when I was feminine and desirable to men. This is an affirmation. I may be back here, but I can't go back to being invisible. Stubbing out my cigarette, my cheeks flush crimson and I wonder who else outside the pub heard. All my paranoia and anxiety has been vindicated in one silly heckle.

Later that night, drinking in a booth as terrible karaoke renditions of 'Caledonia' fill the air, my friends say they don't mind that I'm bisexual, implying they've talked about it amongst themselves. Then they ask which gender I would pick over the other if I had to, and if I've ever had a threesome. I ignore these questions and tell them about the catcallers. Molly looks shocked for a second, then reassures me that I'm still pretty. Would I like to borrow her lipstick? Then the conversation reverts back to their boyfriends. I tune out. We're not on the same page any more, not even in the same library.

These Saturday nights in Foxes make up that summer, between shifts at the café and arguing with my mum about politically correct terms. The people in the pubs are still good and I still like hanging out with them, after a bottle of wine and two pints. Every week at closing time, Molly finds Danny in the crowd and invites me to an after-party with them. Every time I ask her who will be there, she mentions Andy's name, and I hug her goodnight and get a £20 taxi home to Culloden Moor alone.

What I fail to tell Molly when she asks for my gossip from Glasgow is that I have still never been able to enjoy sex, and my body freezes up every time someone comes near it, and I only sleep with people when I'm drunk or high out of my mind. I don't tell her about Andy, and I know a year on that he's not the whole problem. The problem is all the hazy memories of violated boundaries and creeping hands, all the stories of my friends who've been through the same thing, the mundane frequency of it all, the people who think we should shut up about it.

I can't trust my body to give me pleasure. I can't set boundaries for myself now they've all been torn up.

Three months pass, then my dad drives me south down the A9 to Glasgow with my boxes, two weeks before classes restart. The new flat I've found with my friends on Queen Margaret Drive has mould in the bathroom and mice droppings in the kitchen that make my dad tut and sigh as he noses around. I don't care. I dump my belongings in the biggest bedroom and flop down on the creaky mattress, never so relieved to be home.

7. INVERNESS, 2016

CHRISTMAS TIME COMES around again, as it always does, alongside winter, the perpetual depressant. This year I don't book a train home for the holidays because I'm already there. The long nights compound my already tangible boredom. I find myself zoning out of conversations, even with Kathy, and ignoring my mum's attempts to cheer me up with offers of manicures and rom-coms. She has an endless well of patience for my mood swings. Whenever she finds me in the living room, head in hands, book on lap, she says, 'Don't say the B-word! You're too clever a girl to get bored!'

But bored I get. Worse than the restlessness of my teen years, more like an existential exhaustion. Bored of waking up day-to-day and all the mundane mental and bodily functions that go with it. I write poems in the back of my diary, trying to romanticise my quarter-life crisis, but they never see the light of day. I dye my hair more vivid shades of red. Glasgow starts to feel like a dream, and I lose contact with uni friends as I realise I'm obsessed with their lifestyles, which always seem more appealing than mine, no matter how much they complain about difficult masters' degrees or council tax payments.

Why didn't I decide to be a lawyer, or an accountant, or a vet, something useful that pays well? Why wasn't I born into an upper-middle class family in London with contacts in the art world? Why don't my passions align with capitalism? These are the questions I ask myself daily as I sit quietly crying in the office, listening to emo-punk bands through headphones, a few feet away from oblivious Dave. One of my preferred ways to pass time in the office involves googling various mental illnesses and diagnosing myself with them. I scroll through the list of symptoms on the Wikipedia page and mentally check off all the ones I experience. *Lack of enjoyment in things you usually like.* Check. *Inability to perform routine tasks.* Check. *Unfounded sense of terror or dread.* Check, check, check.

One evening in December my dad invites me to a festive dinner at his house with his latest girlfriend, who I've never met. Such forced occasions put me on edge but I have no better plans for tonight. He picks me up from work and we drive through town to the outskirts on the opposite side, where he lives in a cottage in the country with a garden overrun by weeds and stray cats. After he left home when I was a toddler, he moved to London to try and make it as a musician. We didn't see him for a while, but my granddad from the west coast was often around in his place, before he got too sick to visit. Since Dad moved back up north in my pre-teen years to teach saxophone, we have mostly bonded over fantasy novels and astrology. I don't think of him as a parent, so much as a strange middle-aged friend, but I appreciate his bumbling presence in my life. I stopped caring about his love life after he broke up with his long-term ex-partner Iris, a grey-haired hippy who talked to me at length about second-wave feminism in my formative years. Alas, he still refuses to pass on her email address to me.

Halfway to his house, we've covered the obligatory catch-up part of the conversation, and he turns down the volume of the jazz playing on the car stereo.

'I've found someone interested in buying your granddad's house,' he says.

'Oh?' I say, thinking this day would never come. He always saves awkward conversations for the car.

'Young couple from Dornoch looking for something on the coast. They know all about the crofting laws and have some relatives in the area. I went to school with one of their dads, in fact. Never liked him much.'

'When will they be moving in do you think?' I keep my voice casual and pick cat hairs from my jeans.

'It'll take a while if they go ahead with the sale, and I have to fix the leak and the woodworm before they move in. But they viewed the place last weekend,' he says, coming to a stop in rush-hour traffic.

'Ah, I didn't realise that's why you were going up there.'

'I didn't want to tell you too much in case the whole thing fell through, but it went well in the end and now they're just waiting on their own house sale to go through. And mercury should be out of retrograde by then, which is better for signing contracts, of course.' He turns right at a roundabout. 'Just going to nip into the shop to get some things, won't take long. Are you still vegan?'

I nod. He turns to glance at me and I try to blink away the tears in my eyes without being obvious. I feel like such a child. I never cry in front of my dad. He wouldn't know what to do if I did.

'I know it won't be easy to say goodbye to that place, with all the memories attached to it. But it really is just a drain, and money isn't easy right now. Your mum sold her dad's house just a few months after he died.'

'I didn't spend time there though, did I?' I snap. 'It's really sad, to be honest, Dad. I thought the cottage would be around for longer.'

He pulls into a parking spot in the supermarket car park and kills the engine. As if he could sell off my childhood like that. The nerve.

'Inverkirkaig will still be there,' he says, like he's heard me, grabbing his tweed jacket and opening the door. 'You can always camp.'

8. INVERKIRKAIG, 2016

HOGMANAY, IN MY dead granddad's cottage on the north-west coast of the Highlands, with Kathy. Since Dad confirmed the sale of this place, I've been building up to a farewell trip, and after the intensity of Christmas with my mum's extended family – the bickering, the what-are-you-doing-with-your-life talk, the alcohol – I needed to get away. I would have come here alone if I could drive, but Kathy offers to take us in her dad's car, so we travel up the road in the afternoon, stopping in the tourist town of Ullapool halfway to get chips and walk by the pier at sunset. When we reach Lochinver, the nearest village to the cottage, the weather turns. The rain falls in an unrelenting drizzle, grey clouds obscuring the view of the sea, hills, and heather of Inverkirkaig at twilight.

The house smells the same as always, the smell of

every school holiday of my childhood. Nothing much about it has changed since granddad died, except the sense of emptiness that gets bigger as time passes. I make a fire in the living room as soon as we arrive and continue to prod at it with the poke every ten minutes to make the flames dance and feel the heat on my face. Kathy makes a big pan of pasta while I pour drinks and wander around the few rooms of the cottage, checking for spiders and peering into drawers for mementos. My granny's diaries have gone from the bedroom's dresser, I notice, maybe taken by another curious cousin and not returned. I never met her, but I pored over those notebooks. She mostly writes about going to the pictures and birdwatching.

Now we sit around the fire, warm and well-fed. Joni Mitchell croons on the old CD player. I swill whisky around in my tumbler, wishing I liked the taste more. I ask Kathy if she has any resolutions for the New Year.

'Oh, you know,' she says without thinking, 'eat more vegetables, read more books.'

Classic Capricorn. 'Come on, Kat, you must have something more exciting than that.'

She's curled up on the armchair opposite in a long plaid shirt and black velvet leggings, with her hair in a braid to one side, flyaway black hairs around her ears and face. She applies some lip balm and takes several sips of wine before saying, 'Well, Jack called me last week. He says he has some time off this summer before he starts his research placement. He asked if I want to go to Poland with him.'

'That's amazing!' I say. 'You should go!'

She doesn't smile. 'Yeah. It's been, like, for ever since I went. I don't remember it.'

'Would you be able to visit family?' I know next to nothing about Kathy's mum and her relatives. She told me once that she can't miss what she never had.

She rolls her eyes. 'I have no idea. It's not as simple as that. We don't know them. We don't speak any Polish. Jack has all these plans, but he won't follow through . . . Ugh, it's just not realistic.'

I refill my glass. 'I reckon you should go.'

She pauses, then snaps, 'Do you want to look after my dad while I'm gone then, Alice?'

'What?' I say. 'Oh. But surely there's someone who could . . .'

'You don't get it,' she says, getting up to toss more coal onto the fire.

My period has just arrived, explaining the irritable mood I've been in all week, and I bite my tongue before I snap back at her. The tension sends tremors through the tranquil scene. Bringing her here might have been a mistake, inviting her in too deep before either of us are ready.

'Sorry. I guess I don't.' I pick at some paint stuck to the leg of my dungarees. I hum along to the CD, feeling my cheeks burn from the fire, the whisky, the mood. She sits back down on her armchair and I try to fill the silence. 'So no outlandish resolutions. What about the past year then, what are you grateful for?'

Kathy stares into the fire. I want to coax her out from that hole deep inside her head, back to here and to me. I don't know where she goes, what her personal void looks like, and I'm not sure I can pull her out without falling into one myself. After a while she says, 'I don't know, you go first.'

'All right. I'm grateful I made it to the end of uni without dropping out or failing,' I say. 'Even if my degree means fuck all in the harsh light of day.'

'Yeah. Anything else?' she asks, turning in her seat to face me, some kind of challenge in her eyes.

I go over to her, perch on the armrest with my legs on her lap and run her braid through my hand.

'You,' I say. 'I'm thankful for you.'

She draws me in close so my legs are wrapped

around her and the chair threatens to tip backwards. Our chests press into each other. She sighs as I kiss her neck slowly, down to her bare shoulder, pushing aside her shirt and inhaling her warm scent. Her fingers run under my top, up over my waist and towards my chest. We kiss for a while, and just as I am about to unbutton her shirt she breaks away.

Her breath warms my skin and with closed eyes, she murmurs, 'Why don't you show me?'

I run my fingers through her hair until her braid comes loose. The CD spins to its end. 'What do you mean?'

Her forehead presses into me and she speaks down towards my thighs. 'I wish you would show me that you care.'

'I do care,' I say, stroking her head like she's a child who needs comforting. 'I just told you. I care about you so much.'

'Then am I your girlfriend?' she asks, lifting her head to look at me. 'Are you in love with me?' Her eyes look so sad, I want to say *yes, yes* immediately just to make them light up, but my chest goes all tight and I can't bring myself to speak. 'I just need some commitment, Alice,' she says. 'I feel like you're so distant sometimes. I don't want to be held at arm's length for ever.'

I take her hands in mine and clasp and unclasp our fingers, palm to palm.

'I didn't know you felt that way,' I say. 'I'm sorry.' Why must she do this now? If she cared about the stars at all she would know my moon is in Libra and I hate any non-political conflict on a dispositional level. If it was up to me, we would resolve these things telepathically or we would not resolve them at all. We would just go on with our lives, pretending to be fine. I reach around for my glass and take a drink. She doesn't speak. 'I've just never had a relationship this intense before. I never had what you had with Sid.'

'Are you jealous of me and Sid?' she says, shuffling beneath me until I get the hint and move back to the other chair.

'No! No, I swear I'm not jealous, I know you're past that. It's been over a year,' I say, defensive. It never occurred to me to be jealous.

She refills her wine glass, tipping out the final drops, then raises her voice a tad. 'What is it then? I can't mess around with you, Alice, I need more than that. We've spent all our time together for nearly four months.' She keeps going even as I will her to stop. 'Am I too *Inverness* for you?'

'Where is this coming from?' I say, weakly.

'Maybe you're embarrassed by me?' she says, slurring slightly. 'I'm not attacking you, I just need to understand it. I know those types, Alice, who string people along for company and sex until they get bored, but I know you're not one of them.'

I try my best to keep calm. 'I have to pee then smoke a cigarette, then we can talk more,' I say, getting up to leave. I stand out in the foggy front garden, smoking quickly in the dead quiet as my fingers freeze. Moisture glistens on the grass in the shadows of the cottage. Our first fight! What a shitty milestone. She doesn't drink this much very often. Maybe that's all it is. Or maybe I need to get my shit together and give her a reason to stay with me, if I want her to.

When I return, she's sitting cross-legged on the floor, reading a book from the shelf about birdlife in the Highlands, flicking through the pages of sparrows and hawks absent-mindedly.

'Hey,' I say, sitting down on the chair. 'Sorry I made you feel that way, like I was stringing you along. I have intimacy issues or something, whatever, I don't know.'

'Sometimes we have to move past our traumas to get close to other people, Alice,' she says without looking up. 'Everyone does it.'

I nearly laugh, but summon some maturity and say, 'Thank you for sticking around anyway. And for being so patient with all my weird insecurities about sex and everything. And sorry for turning this around to be about me, again . . .' I stop and try to read her silent face. 'I really like you and I want you to feel valued in this – in our relationship.'

'Okay,' she says, getting up to sit on the chair. Is this how couple arguments work, I wonder? One person says how they feel, then the other feeds them platitudes until they feel guilty for starting it and nothing changes? 'Sorry for snapping at you here. I know coming was important to you. We can talk about it more another time. I was up so early today, I need to sleep. But I do love you, you know.'

Oh god. That's a new one. Before I have to form a reply, I notice the time on the old brass clock on the mantelpiece. 'Kathy, we missed the bells. It's after twelve. Happy New Year.'

'Happy New Year,' she says, coming over to hug

me. I receive her and hold her tight. We stay like that for a long time, perfectly still in the hug, her face buried into my shoulder, the fire crackling behind us.

New Year's morning. I wake up early with Kathy sleeping beside me, lying on her side, lips parted and stained purple from wine. The room falls into place around me. I roll over gently so as not to wake her, smell the musty wool blanket, and see the green neon numbers on the radio alarm: 06:55. I need to pee and my throat is parched, so I slip out of bed to the bathroom. I empty my menstrual cup, enjoying the gory sight of blood filling the toilet bowl, then drink some water from the tap and splash my face with cold water.

When I get to the living room, I feel the embers of the fire still emitting a little warmth. *White rabbit*, I mutter out loud to myself for good luck when I remember it's the first day of the month, a superstition passed on from my great-aunt, who once lived in the cottage on the other side of the croft. I switch on the table lamp. Our dishes sit beside it, unwashed. My head feels heavy and hot all of a sudden. I might be residually drunk but I want fresh air, so I pick up a jumper and pull on my jacket and wellies, a pack of cigarettes and a lighter, then head out the back door, closing it quietly.

All is dark, no light pollution for miles, but the sunrise tints the skyline with a pale blue-green, and a new moon hangs over the bay. I feel the cold come to rest on the exposed parts of my skin and breathe in the rich air. Letting my eyes adjust to the pre-dawn, I crunch over the gravel to the gate and close it behind me so the roaming sheep don't get into the garden. I set off down the single-track road around the edge of the family croft towards Inverkirkaig bay. Halfway down, I spot a shadowy movement on the tarmac at my feet. On closer inspection, it's a toad, frozen still before me. Shining, grey, perfectly camouflaged in concrete. I admire its weird shining form, then walk on, resisting the urge to pick it up and watch it wriggle in my hands.

I pass my late great-aunt's house and make it to the beach. Rugged hills envelope the bay on both sides, and the high tide laps quietly at the rocks. I cross the grassy bank and pick my way across the rocks to the water. Overnight, the clouds have cleared to show off the last faint glow of stars, as light rises. The first sun of the year. In the mouth of the bay between the two points to the west, the sky meets the sea and the waves glint in the dark.

Feeling fully awake with the energy of the land, I start to clamber across the beach to the rocks down the right-hand side of the bay. I'm gripped by the desire to see the whole horizon, the one visible from the end of the point, uninterrupted by claustrophobic hills, sure that only then will I be able to breathe properly, only when I reach the open sea will the year begin, only then will I make sense of it all. Foot after foot, hand after hand, crossing seaweed and barnacles and heather, full of memories of my smaller body gallivanting over these rocks like a mountain goat. My fitness doesn't match my determination, but I persevere through the breathlessness, focus on not missing a step, until I look up into the familiar brightening landscape and see the horizon. The whole sea stretches out in front of me, Inverkirkaig behind, no houses in sight from here on these craggy cliffs, just me and the sky and the open sea and the hills at my back.

I let out a laugh of relief and sit down on a flat bit of rock to catch my breath. If I slipped over the ledge just below me, I would tumble over the seaweed-covered rocks and into the deep sea to meet my fate down with the basking sharks. Imagine if my foot slipped. Imagine if I fell. What would the moment of impact feel like, falling into the iron abyss, slapped by waves? Suddenly everything around me is illuminated and I look back to take in the sun appearing through the hills of Assynt, my cottage hidden by the land I've crossed to get here, to my favourite spot.

With my freezing hands, I light a cigarette and sit smiling out to the morning. Here I am, alone, happier than I've been in months and months. Delirious with happiness, in fact! Look out there at that view, I think to myself. West! I want to go west, take a voyage like my ancestors after the Highland Clearances, but without the violent colonialism, go transatlantic, see larger versions of this landscape and write about *them*, fly on a plane alone and change my name and make a new life from scratch. I have to go. New Year's resolution: get out. Can't be that hard. I stub out my cigarette and, after a moment's moral conflict, wrap it in a tissue and put it in my pocket.

I realise my bum and legs have gone numb as I stand up and reach out to the heather above the rock to steady myself. Must get back. I pull my scarf up over my face to protect from the wind whipping up from the water. What a long way I've walked.

Is Kathy awake yet? Will she worry? Will she have left in the car, driven back to Inverness, leaving me here to live alone, uncontactable and free to do what I please as a hermit?

About forty-five minutes later, I reach the road and the cottage comes into view. The car is gone. My chest goes tight and I pick up the pace, powering up the hill. When I get there, any notions that the car might be parked behind the house, that she might have moved it, are dispelled. No car. I go into the kitchen through the back door that's never locked.

'Kathy?' No response. I kick off my wellies and gulp water from a glass left out on the side, parched from the walk. I turn up the heating, then walk through the quiet house, noting that her jacket is gone from the hanger in the hallway, but her toothbrush still sits in the bathroom. Would she really leave like that? Did I scare her by going out so early? She could be out looking for me. Fuck.

I slump down in an armchair in the sun lounge, still wearing my jacket, and stare out of the glass doors to the garden and over the croft at the cool, clear morning. A couple of minutes later, the kitchen door opens, making me jump.

'Kathy? Is that you?' I rush towards the back door.

'Morning, Alice. Of course it's me. Who did you think it was?' She frowns at the panicked expression on my face. 'We didn't take any milk, so I drove to Lochinver to see if the shop was open.'

So obvious. 'I thought you ... never mind. Sorry. Happy New Year.' I lean in to kiss her cocoa butter lips, wrap my arms around her baggy black hoodie, sad that I thought the worst of her. She pulls away and goes to put on the kettle.

'It was weird waking up alone earlier,' she says, moving my wellies out of the way and looking up and down at my pyjama bottoms and jacket combo. God, she makes me self-conscious sometimes. 'Especially in this creaky house. Where did you go?'

'Sorry,' I say, clearing dishes from the counter and looking out breakfast foods. 'I went for a walk. Woke up really early and knew I wouldn't be able to sleep, so I walked along the bay to see the sunrise ... it was beautiful.'

'Fair enough,' she says, going through to the living room and gathering up last night's dishes. 'Maybe you should shower.'

We pass a tense morning in the cottage, eating and reading and not talking much, then the rain starts up, scuppering our plans for an afternoon walk. New

Year's Day nausea kicks in around noon. I wander around the cottage, whispering goodbyes to each room, resisting the temptation to scratch my name into the furniture. We clear out and drive back to Inverness.

9. INVERNESS, 2017

SUNDAY, MIDDAY, KATHY'S bed. Her dad is away visiting her aunt in Aberdeen so we have the place to ourselves. Sleepy in her arms with sunlight streaming in through the blinds, I wake up, take in her hair on the pillow, her leg beneath mine, the old band posters on the wall. Thinking about last night, it occurs to me how nice it would be to wake up like this every single morning, for ever. But I can't. Guilt settles in, gets comfortable for the day ahead. She rolls over and smiles at me. Her freckles are emerging in the early spring.

I get up to make coffee and brunch. In the kitchen, measuring out flour into a bowl, I say, 'I usually use bananas instead of eggs to make vegan pancakes, do you have any?'

She leans over and kisses my shoulder. 'My god, you're so *Glasgow*.'

'Fuck off!' I say and pull her in towards me, covering her black T-shirt in flour. In my head, *tell her tell her end it tell her* whizzes back and forth and back and forth. But I don't, yet. Everything seems perfect when you're about to give it up.

She turns to put on music. We dance around the kitchen to Beyoncé until I've piled two plates with pancakes, which we take back to bed to eat. She opens the curtains as we eat to look out the window. 'It's sunny, Alice! We should go out.'

Half an hour later, we're in her dad's old red Volkswagen Polo on the road to Nairn beach, pulling into the wee seaside town, passing the chippies and charity shops and arguing over whether the east or west beach is better. She pulls into the first car park we find. We pause as the engine shuts down and the radio goes silent, facing out to sea. A raincloud hangs in the distance, threatening the blue sky above.

'Race you,' she says, opening the door and bolting out of the car, looking back to taunt me. I stall for a second, then grab my jacket, jump out after her and run across the car park past a group of boys on skateboards, across the grassy verge and onto the wet sand.

She shrieks ahead of me, her long legs flicking

out around her dark hair whipping in the wind like a mane. I pant, laughing, as we run down to the sea where the tide is far out, exposing seaweed and stones on the sand for metres ahead of us. She stops to kick off her Doc Martens and I copy.

'You hard enough for this?' she says, all glinting eyes and rosy cheeks and *I'm-from-further-north-than-you* bravado.

'Of course!' I say, whipping my jeans down to my ankles and kicking them off.

We both strip, grinning at each other like competitive sisters, taking off jackets, then jumpers, then T-shirts, until we stand beside each other, me in my sports bra and knickers, Kathy in a lacy black bra and pants, and I grab her hand.

'FUCK!' she yells as the cold wind whips around our bare skin and our feet splash into the shallows. I scream as the first wave crashes above my knees, and run ahead to turn and look at her, dancing backwards through the waves as she comes towards me.

'Ohmygod, Alice!'

We keep going in, further and deeper, oblivious to the teenage boys in the car park squinting down at us and the raincloud closing in, blocking out the sun. I can hear my heartbeat in my ears, my nose runs, and when the icy water hits my vaginal area, I stop breathing for a second.

'Oh shit, oh shit, oh shit!' She splashes over to me, breathless. We kiss each other hard with freezing lips that taste of salt. I cling to her wet skin, unable to catch my breath.

'To the horizon!' I yell. I dive down into the water and swim, plunging my head into the cold oblivion of the North Sea. Everything stops. When I come up for air, she's still there, shining wet in the waves.

Half an hour later, we sit in the car in a parking spot on the high street, wriggling about in our jeans with no underwear beneath them. She's turned the heat up full and the Top 40 plays on the radio as we pass a portion of vinegar-soaked chips between us and watch the rain start to patter down onto the windshield. I feel elated from the swim and exhausted from the laughing and nervous about what I have to do next.

'Kathy, I have some news.'

'Oh yeah? Are you pregnant?'

'Hah . . . ha . . . well,' I swallow a chip and apply some of the lip balm she offers me. 'I think I'm leaving Inverness soon.'

'Oh. Are you applying for a master's?'

'No. I'm applying for a visa,' I say, looking out of the window ahead, trying to be casual. 'For Canada.'

'Canada?' She turns around in her seat to face me. 'What the fuck, Alice? That's huge! What for?'

'Just to work for a while, I suppose? I know it's kind of far . . . but it'd be for a year, maybe two, I'd try and write, get a job in a bar, make some friends . . . It'd be really cool if you came to visit.'

'Canada. Where? Which part?'

'Toronto, probably. There are some cousins there I've never met . . .'

She goes quiet. After a while, staring out of the window through a clear patch in the fogged-up glass, she says, 'I knew you wouldn't last here long.' Her voice is flat. 'See the world while you're young and all that. When are you going?'

'Probably summer. I haven't booked a flight or anything yet. There's still some paperwork to send off and then I should have the visa by April—'

'Why didn't you tell me before?' she interrupts.

'I didn't think I'd do it! I didn't want to make a big deal out of it then fail. It was just an idea.'

'What am I going to do when you leave?' she says in a small voice, her jaw tightening.

'You'll be completely fine, Kathy. You won't be here for ever.'

After a pause, she says, 'But that's not the point.'

We drive back to Inverness in silence. She has this way of going quiet. Usually I hate silence, but I can't bring myself to break hers. When she drops me off at my mum's house, she only kisses me on the cheek.

10. INVERNESS, 2017

THE EMAIL FROM Canadian immigration services loads slowly.

> You have received a new message about your application #D10657.

I click through to the website and then on the inbox icon. Another window pops up, a list of opened messages appears, topped by one unread message.

> Update on your application #D10657.

My heart beats fast as I try to maintain a calm exterior for my mum, who sits on the other side of the room painting her toenails on the armchair. *Load. Come on, fucking load.*

Your application for the IEC Working Holiday Visa (2017 pool) has been successful. Please send the documents listed below so we can process your visa within 10 weeks.

'Fuck,' I say aloud. Mum looks up, frowns, then looks back at her feet. I can go. If I find a cheap flight . . . I could be there by May. I open the calculator app on my computer and work out how much I'll earn over the next two months, and open a flight booking website in a new tab.

Toronto Pearson, May 15th, economy class, one-way.

I find the letter sitting in the hallway by the front door when I go to run a bath on Friday night. Weird, I think, mum usually gets to the post first. I pick it up and recognise the handwriting, the simple letters of my first name etched across the centre of the envelope. Kathy must have driven up in her car and delivered it this evening. We haven't spoken since lunchtime on Wednesday, when she stormed out of Starbucks mid-conversation and I didn't follow her. I'd been half-heartedly suggesting she come with me to Toronto, but she saw right through the façade to the part of me that was saying: *we're breaking up*. I take the letter through to the living room and sit down on the sofa, petting Moss as she jumps up on my lap and mews.

'Yes, Moss, you're right. It's from Kathy. What do you think she's going to say? You like Kathy, don't you, Mossy-girl?' I rip along the seal and take out the single page of lined paper. Such beautiful hand-writing! The looped e's and neatly dotted i's make me miss her. 'What have I done, Moss-girl? Should I stay? What do you think?'

The cat rubs her soft face into my hand and purrs, her claws extending into the skin of my thighs through my leggings and making me wince.

Dear Alice,
I love you but you have places to go without me and I can't wait around at your side while you bide your time here. You know I can't come with you and I know you don't really want me to. Please don't read this letter as cold, I'm just trying to be rational, and it's easier to do that when you're not sitting in front of me. Give me a week or two, then if you want to meet up and talk about it, that's fine. I'm not going anywhere fast. Thank you

for everything and for reminding me I'm still young. Don't feel obliged to respond to this if you need time to think.

I miss you already but I know we have to do this,

Love Kathy

xoxo

Hot tears drip down onto the paper and I cling onto Moss as I scan the single side of text again and again. None of this felt real until now. I hope she didn't cry as she wrote this. I hope she feels confident that we're better apart. But really I hope she's falling apart without me. Maybe I'm a terrible person.

Just then, Mum walks in through the kitchen door.

'Oh! Hello, Alice, hello, Moss. I didn't expect you to be in,' she says, as I dry my face roughly with my sleeve and stuff the letter under a cushion. Mum dumps her shopping bags on the table and looks at me. 'Are you all right?'

'I'm fine, Mum!' The hungry cat hops off my lap and runs over to circle Mum's feet. 'Staying in tonight, not going to Kathy's this week.'

Since I started dating Kathy, Mum has become an unexpectedly casual ally, never asking questions but always appearing calm when I bring her up. Sometimes she even tags me in news stories about LGBT rights on Facebook.

'Oh, a night in for us both then,' she says, unpacking the groceries. 'Would you like a cup of tea? I'm putting the kettle on. Maureen's coming over later, you know, Maureen from Balloch. She's excited to hear more about your big news . . .'

I nod as she chatters away, swallowing a sob and getting up to go to the bathroom. I spend most of the evening crying in the bath, only crawling out when Maureen needs to pee.

The following Friday night I tag along with Molly to Foxes for the first time in months. We knock back a shot of tequila each, and go to a booth by the window with our pints to claim a spot before it fills up.

'So you broke up with her? Or she broke up with you?' asks Molly, taking out a compact mirror and dusting her face with shimmering bronze powder.

'Can I have some of that?' She passes me the make-up. I applied extra eyeshadow and mascara before coming out tonight to discourage myself from weeping in the toilets. 'I guess it was mutual. Doesn't make it easier though. I feel so stupid, like I set all of this up to happen, and now I'm an emotional wreck . . .'

'You'll forget about it once you're away though. Danny did this to me at the end of last year,' she says, matter-of-factly. 'Threatened to move to Australia with Andy—'

'Andy moved to Australia?'

'Keep up, Alice. This is what happens when you never reply to my texts!'

'Fair,' I say, inspecting my bronzed cheeks in the mirror.

'Anyway, so he got cold feet just before we moved in together and was all, "We're too young for this!" – even though he's ten years older than me, but whatever – and I was shitting it for a while that he was going to leave, then we didn't speak for like a week. He went on a massive bender, then came crawling back and said sorry a week later. Said he wasn't thinking straight and it made him remember how much he loves me.'

I gulp down my Tennent's, waiting for her to go on, but now she's checking her phone, probably for messages from Danny.

'Right,' I say. 'Are you suggesting I'm going to run back to Kathy?'

She smiles at her iPhone screen, then looks up, 'What?'

'I don't know how that— Never mind.'

'Here, there's Murray from my work, remember him from school? Murray! Over here!'

I drain my pint glass and brace myself for the evening, excusing myself to smoke as Murray bombards Molly with a bear hug and starts to regale her with a tale of the bouncer he punched last week.

'They told me I was barred, but look who's laughing now, eh!'

Note to self: book flight tomorrow.

I wake up in Kathy's bed on the first of May. The smell of the sheets is so familiar and soothing that for a moment I forget the situation, relishing the sensations of a safe, protected place. Meeting to talk in the evening was a mistake, perhaps one we both wanted to make. We took a taxi from the rank near the restaurant at midnight without talking about the fact that I was getting out at her place in the suburbs and we were going straight to her bedroom. We didn't talk about the fact that she started silently crying immediately after sex, or that I pretended to immediately fall asleep. Now, in the morning light, my lethargic mind sorts through options: try and leave before she wakes up, never speak again; wake her up and say goodbye; go back to sleep and hope she goes out somewhere before I wake up; stay for breakfast and face a horribly awkward conversation; stay for ever in her affection and put all the money I spent on a one-way flight in two weeks' time down to trial and error.

After a while, Kathy stirs beside me. I consider playing dead but I'm too late, she rolls over and clocks me.

'Morning, Alice,' she mumbles, rubbing her eyes and stretching without touching me.

'Hi,' I mumble back. Cue heavy pause. 'I should go . . . supposed to be going for a walk with my mum today and . . . shit, it's half ten already . . .'

'Do you want coffee before you go? I need some anyway.'

'Don't worry about it, I'll get out of your way.'

I hop out of her bed and open the curtains a crack to let the spring morning stream in, then source my clothes from where they are strewn across the floor. The two jugs of sangria we shared at the tapas bar have left me parched, so I nip to the toilet to pee and drink cold water from the tap. *Goodbye, Kathy's toilet,*

I think, sniffing the scent of her favourite hand soap on my skin for the last time.

She's gone through to the kitchen by the time I get back to her room. I quickly get dressed. She returns with a mug in hand and stands by her bed as I search for my stuff.

'Here you go,' she says, passing me the battered black bag from a spot by her feet.

'Thanks,' I say.

'Have safe travels,' she says.

'I'll try. Take care of yourself.'

We both smile a little at the forced platitudes. I turn towards the door of her immaculate childhood bedroom. She follows, and we hug each other for a brief tight moment.

'Bye then.'

'I can send you a postcard if you want.'

'Sure,' she says, opening the back door for me. The last time I see her she's standing in the doorway in her red dressing gown, black hair tied up in a topknot, eyeliner smudged around her eyes. As soon as I get past her gate and hear the door close behind me, the tears come thick and fast. I walk down the cul-de-sac, past kids playing in manicured gardens and cats perched in windowsills, sobbing for all the things

I didn't say. When I reach the end of her street, I instinctively take the back path by the park towards the woods which separate the suburbs from Culloden Moor. The air feels warm on my skin for the first time this year.

The woods calm me down. I find an old tissue at the bottom of my bag and blow my nose, then set off up the path by the railway line which will eventually lead me home. Endless branches obscure the sunlight. I feel the way I have always felt among trees, like a witchy child in a folk tale who might just run off the path and be swept away into a different realm and never speak to another human again. My body craves coffee, but once I get into a rhythm of walking, the oxygen propels me through the hangover, and I smile *hello* to every person and dog I meet, trying not to think about the look on Kathy's face as we parted, or the feel of her skin on mine.

An hour later I make it back to my mum's house, tired, hot and thirsty. No messages from Kathy. I start to compose one to her, then delete it and turn off my phone. I take the letter she wrote to me out of my diary and put it in a book which I place back on the shelf, hoping not to find it again.

11. GOING

SIX A.M., INVERNESS Airport. Everyone moves with an eerie calm as the sun begins to tease the sky outside. My flight to Dublin leaves in an hour and a half, where I'll wait around for six hours until my flight to Toronto, and when I arrive there I'll have been awake for twenty hours already and it won't even be dark yet. Both my parents have come, the second time the three of us have spent time together in ten years. The atmosphere makes me even more eager to get through security. My sleep-deprived brain tunes in and out of the conversation.

'Have you been in touch with your cousins in Ontario, then, Iain?'

'Yes, Carol, I've told Alice all about them. They know she's coming.'

'Good, I'd worry if she didn't have anyone to call in an emergency.'

'Would you like a coffee, Carol?'

'I'll get my own coffee, thanks, Iain. Alice?'

I take my eyes off the departures board for a second. 'Mm? Yes, coffee, that'd be great.'

My mum smiles. She's been threatening to cry all morning but I hope to make my escape before it comes to that. The sadness will hit me later and I'll phone her in a mess. For now I can only feel anxiety buzzing through all my organs like an electric current.

'You'd better have some caffeine before your flight or you won't make it on board!' she says, handing some coins to my dad, who wanders off to the only café in the airport. I message Quinn, confirming my arrival time. They've promised to take me for food in Chinatown when I get into the city. I've promised to bring them a bottle of Irn Bru.

Dad returns at six-fifteen with three black coffees. I put aside the travel documents in my hand and try to be nice for another ten minutes. Mum tells me she can send thermals in winter, and Dad tells me to try meditating on the plane to keep calm. I nod and smile. When the moment comes for me to go through security, the final barrier, I hug them both in a daze, squeezing my mum tighter as she gets emotional. I pull my rucksack over my shoulders and lug my case towards the next room. One last wave, and I'm gone.

I make it through security without beeping. In the small perfume shop in the departures lounge, I spray some Chanel on my wrists, then go and claim a bench in the waiting area. More alone than I've ever been, suddenly wide awake, a huge grin spreads over my face. I look out through the windows onto the runway and the sun rising behind it. Here goes.

Acknowledgements

Thank you to my family and friends for the books, love and support.

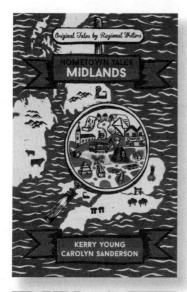